SKI

MAGAZINE'S Guide

To New England & Quebec

BY THE EDITORS OF
SKI Magazine

EDITED BY
Moira McCarthy

MOUNTAIN SPORTS PRESS

Boulder, Colorado USA

SKI Magazine's Guide to New England and Quebec

Published by Mountain Sports Press

Distributed to the book trade by
PUBLISHERS GROUP WEST

Copyright © 2003 Mountain Sports Media

Bill Grout, Editor-in-Chief
Michelle Klammer Schrantz, Art Director
Scott Kronberg, Associate Art Director
Chris Salt, Managing Editor
Alex Pasquariello, Editorial Assistant
Andy Hawk, Account Manager

Cover photo by: Dennis Curran
Contributors: Marty Basch, Stu Campbell, Steve Cohen, Krista Crabtree, Joe Cutts,
Fletcher Doyle, David Green, Linda Hayes, David Healy, Doug Lewis, Moira McCarthy,
Kelley Lewis, Sandy MacDonald, Michael Miracle, Ken Moran, Hilary Nangle,
Richard Needham, Meg Lukens Noonan, Alex Pasquariello, Nathaniel Reade, Bill Rice,
Casey Seiler, Bernadette Starzee, Scott Sutherland, Eric Vohr

ISBN 0-9724827-2-5
Library of Congress Cataloging-in-Publication Data applied for.

First paperback edition. September 2003

Printed in the USA, by RR Donnelley Corporation

CONTENTS

94 NEW YORK

124 QUEBEC

148 VERMONT

Introduction

There's more to skiing in the New England than just sliding down snow-covered mountains. But that's never been a secret to the millions of people who inhabit the metropolises of the Eastern Seaboard. They head north in winter not only for the white-carpeted slopes and the rush of wind in their faces, but for the charm of historic villages and the beauty of forested, rolling countryside.

As you drive northward from cities like Boston, Hartford and New York, six-lane freeways become two-lane highways and then curving secondary roads that are heaved and buckled with frost. In places too steep for agriculture, hardwood forests spill down to the roadside, crowding it with beech, birch, maple and fir. Every five miles or so a village appears with a columned town hall, graceful Victorian homes and steepled churches still standing straight and true on granite foundations laid a century ago. Driving through those villages on frosty winter evenings, mullioned windows glow yellow and warm and inviting.

New England's mountains are ancient even by geological standards. Their once-soaring peaks have been eroded to manageable elevations by ancient ice and then covered with hardwood forests. On these hillsides, skiing's pioneers hacked out wild and wooly trails and found the skiing to be excellent. The only problem was natural snow cover, which was often deep, but sometimes scant. Not so any more. Snowguns and grooming machines have revolutionized Eastern skiing, virtually guaranteeing snow from December to March.

Tiny Vermont remains the skiing capital of the Northeast. Its elder statesmen are Stowe, Sugarbush and Killington, though upstarts like Okemo and Stratton also draw thousands to their slopes. In New Hampshire, the biggest hills, including Loon, Attitash, Cannon and Wildcat, are clustered along the spine of the White Mountains in the northern part of the state. In Maine, wilderness surrounds the skiing outposts of Sunday River and Sugarloaf. Downcountry, the lesser peaks of the Berkshires and Catskills offer terrific day skiing much closer to Boston and New York. And though it's just over the border, Quebec feels a world away—an authentically French experience, right down to the fine food and wine you'd expect.

All over the region, smaller areas offer unique, less crowded and less expensive alternatives well worth exploring—as long as you're careful not to measure the quality of the experience in vertical feet skied or black diamonds conquered. At Quebec's Le Massif, for instance, you can gaze out over the ice-clogged St. Lawrence River from atop the Canadian Shield. In Vermont, you can still ride the rope at Cochran's or explore modern skiing's roots at Suicide Six.

Wherever you go, dress warm: There's a reason those old Yankee farmers have grown so hardy. And be assured that when the sun sets on Northeastern resorts, the fun isn't over. In cheery pubs and fine restaurants, ruddy faced skiers gather round fireplaces and polished bars to share their experiences in laughter and conversation—and to look forward to another day replete with the unique experiences of New England skiing.

–JOE CUTTS
Eastern Editor, SKI Magazine

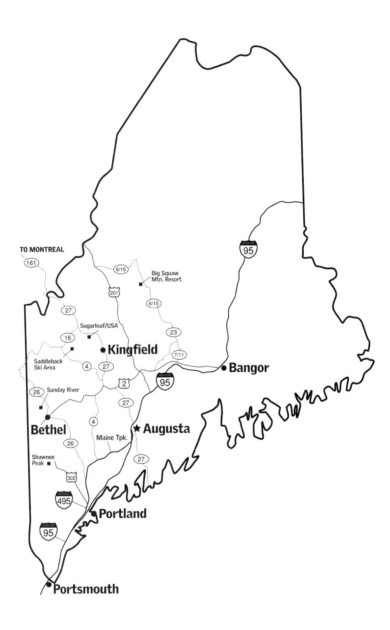

TO MONTREAL
161
6/15
Big Squaw
Mtn. Resort
201
6/15
27
Sugarloaf/USA
16
23
Kingfield
Saddleback
Ski Area
7/11
4 27
Bangor
2
95
26 Sunday River
27
4
Bethel
★ **Augusta**
26 Maine Tpk.
Shawnee
Peak
27
302
495
Portland
95

Portsmouth

95

Maine

SKI MAGAZINE'S GUIDE TO NEW ENGLAND AND QUEBEC

MAINE

Sugarloaf/USA

CARRABASSETT VALLEY, MAINE

Sugarloaf proves once again that life is all a matter of perspective. About the worst thing most *SKI* Magazine readers have to say about Maine's mightiest mountain is that it's "in the absolute middle of nowhere." To its regulars, however—and Sugarloaf is a real regular's mountain—that isolation is part of the appeal: The long drive thins the crowds and weeds out all but those interested foremost in what one *SKI* reader calls "the best pure ski mountain in the East."

Come around "Oh My Gosh" corner on Route 16, and you'll get plenty of perspective: That huge, conical mountain with 2,820 feet of vertical drop (the second-tallest resort in the original colonies) provides what one *SKI* reader calls "the most varied and challenging terrain in the East." The Snowfields at the mountain's summit—open at least half the season—are the only lift-accessed, above-tree-line skiing in the East, and the killer steeps on trails like White Nitro and Upper Winter's Way will keep even the best experts sweaty. Intermediates, meanwhile, can find an entire day of undisturbed cruising on the wide-open slopes off the Wiffletree SuperQuad™.

Sugarloaf gets high marks for its staff, restaurants, snowmaking, and grooming. "The type of place where everyone knows your name," one *SKI* reader cheers. The weather is more debatable. Some argue that it can get particularly cold here, but others respond that that's why Sugarloaf gets powder when other resorts get rain. And when readers complain that it's hard to get to, Sugarloaf cognoscenti respond: Not if you're already there. —N.R.

VITAL STATS

SUMMIT: 4,237 feet

VERTICAL DROP: 2,820 feet

SKIABLE ACRES: 1,400

BEGINNER: 27%

INTERMEDIATE: 30%

ADVANCED/EXPERT: 43%

SNOWMAKING: 92% coverage

AVG. ANNUAL SNOWFALL: 240 in.

LIFTS: 15; 2 SuperQuads™, 2 high-speed quads, 8 doubles, 1 triple, 2 surface lifts

TERRAIN PARKS/HALFPIPES: 1 terrain park, 1 halfpipe

INFO: 800-THE-LOAF; www.sugarloaf.com

SKIING IT

With seven of the resort's 15 lifts within walking distance of the base lodge, everything at Sugarloaf starts and ends in the same spot. The easiest

Isolation is part of the appeal for regulars who enjoy Sugarloaf's powder and ski-in ski-out village.

terrain flanks the village, offering favorites like beginner-friendly Birches, accessible off the Snubber Triple Chair, and the Family Fun parks the Wiffletree. Sugarloaf's east side is home to the area's toughest terrain, including the Snowfields and King Pine Bowl. If it's groomers and cruisers you want, stick to the Loaf's large central section.

The Sugarloaf SuperQuad™ high speed and centrally located, provides access to almost everything on the mountain. It bisects Competition Hill and the bump-laden Skidder trail, and delivers quick trips to many of Sugarloaf's 36 intermediate runs. For classic New England skiing, head west off the SuperQuad™ to the West Mountain and Bucksaw doubles. For a scenic cruiser, head east off the quad to the Rookie River glade, which follows a creek bed and has such spacing between trees you'll think you're out West.

Snowmaking covers 92 percent of the mountain, but diehards looking for natural skiing and powder stashes can find it in the Snowfields up above tree line. For mogul addicts, Bubblecuffer, steep and stuffed with bumps, is among the best. Sugarloaf also has hike-to runs off the summit and down the backside to the King Pine Area. For a leg-burning, three-mile cruiser, Tote Road takes you from the top down to the village in 2,820 vertical feet. –K.C.

FAMILY MATTERS

For all the talk about steeps and kick-butt skiing (and it's for real), don't think for a moment that Sugarloaf forgot the rest of the ski equation. They've been intently focusing on family and kids' ski programs for two decades now. In fact, in the past Sugarloaf has been rated above perennial best-for-families winner Smuggler's Notch in a prominent family magazine.

The winning formula? Easy access, great programs, and slopeside lodging. Sugarloaf's daycare center sits at the base of the mountain, where parents can zip by and peek in on their kids on the way to the chair, barely missing a beat. And Sugarloaf was among the first in the ski industry to provide beepers to nursing moms and other parents who might need to stay tied in. The obligatory on-slope costumed characters are there (Amos the Moose is a kiddie favorite), and Sugarloaf offers ski school programs that fit all ages and abilities.

The mountain's layout proves family friendly as well. The winding Tote Road, for example, pops in and out of the mountain's steeper slopes, offering a stress-free yet fun run any family member can take while others get their thrills. The trees are pro-family, too, with Blueberry's Grove Glade the perfect place to show the kids what tree skiing is all about without ever putting them in an uncomfortable situation.

With most of the lodging slopeside—and everything else accessed by a free shuttle—families need never lug equipment around or start the car to get to all the other diversions. The indoor pool, outdoor hot tubs, turbo tubing, ice skating, sleigh rides and the "anti-gravity" complex are all a walk or short shuttle ride away.

GETTING THERE
From Boston

Take I-95 North to Exit 31B. Take Route 27 North through Farmington and Kingfield to Sugarloaf.

Drive Time: 4.5 hours

From Montreal

Take Route 10 East to Route 112 East to Route 253 South. Take Route 253 South to Cookshire and take a left onto Route 108. Take Route 108 to Route 212 East through La Patrie to Woburn. Take Route 161 South to the U.S. border. Sugarloaf is approximately 36 miles south on Route 27.

Drive Time: 4 hours

LODGING

A wide selection of accommodations falls under the umbrella of Sugarloaf Central Lodging (800-THE-LOAF). They range from casual to frills, but all are comfortable. They include:

Sugarloaf boasts Maine's second highest peak and the East's only lift-accessed, above-tree-line skiing.

Grand Summit Resort Hotel

A world-class, full-service hotel that evokes the style and spirit of a classic mountain lodge. Located at the top end of the village, the Hotel is convenient to lifts and all the village hot spots. The most hotel-like of the choices, it has valet parking, concierge service and rooms of varying sizes.

Gondola Village Condominiums

Clustered near lifts and activities throughout the village, the condos range in size from one to five bedrooms, and most have fireplaces and balconies or decks overlooking the slopes.

Sugarloaf Inn

Comfortable, country-style, and close to the action, with everything you need and nothing you don't. This Inn is the more basic choice at the Loaf, and sits right next to the health club and a chairlift.

The Herbert Grand Hotel
Kingfield, Maine

With its pressed-tin ceilings and grand piano, the Herbert is a classic example of the kind of "grand" hotel that could once be found throughout New England. Dating back to 1917, the look is dark oak, brass fixtures and terrazzo floors. It must be one of the last places in America where you can still find writing tables with stationery and flower-filled vases in the halls on each floor. But thanks to several updatings, most of the 27 rooms boast jacuzzi tubs. And the new owners, Marcie and Lynn Herrick, plan further improvements. Sugarloaf/USA lies 20 minutes north, and at day's end, you can relax on a velvet couch in front of the fire with a drink before heading into the award-winning restaurant. If you want other dining choices, Kingfield has all the civilization you require in the North Woods. Double rooms are reasonably priced and include continental breakfast. Info: 888-656-9922; www.herbertgrandhotel.com

 DINING
Hug's Italian Cuisine
Carrabassett Valley, Maine

If you sometimes hunger for an old-fashioned Italian restaurant, the kind not ashamed of red sauce and not so relentlessly nouveau, then get your fix at Hug's, a roadside trattoria not far from Sugarloaf. The tiny proportions of this clapboard cottage yield all sorts of cozy nooks, while the portions of food are as big as the place is small—all the more so if you opt for the "family style" dinner. Specialties range from fettuccine Alfredo (in a savory pink variation) to shrimp-and-scallop puttanesca. The closest you'll come to trendy is the shiitake mushroom ravioli, which, like all the luscious pasta here, is handmade. Info: 207-237-2392 —S.M.

Shuck's Grill
Kingfield, Maine

Visiting Maine without having a seafood dinner is like going to Chicago and not ordering beef. The seafood standout at Sugarloaf and a favorite among regulars is Shuck's. The oysters alone are reason enough to come here, but the casual bar and restaurant also offers other seafood in portions to suit any appetite. Appetizers include peel-and-eat shrimp, clam fritters, and Cajun blackened scallops. The Lite Menu is light on price but heavy on the plate, with favorites like the smoked seafood quesadilla, which is a meal unto itself. Entrées are even more substantial. Choose from a thick grilled tuna steak with Thai peanut sauce, a seafood-packed bouillabaisse and macadamia-encrusted swordfish. Landlubbers can opt for hefty burgers as well as steak, lamb and duckling. Reservations are recommended for weekends and holidays. Info: 207-237-2040 —H.N.

The Bag and Kettle
Carrabassett Valley, Maine

Ask any local how long The Bag has been here, and he'll likely scratch his head, hem and haw a little, and then say, "forever." Actually, it's been since 1969, first down in Carrabassett Valley, but with its almost ski-in location next to the base lodge since 1972. Indeed, after a hard morning on the slopes, it's difficult to resist the scent of charbroiled burgers wafting from The Bag. If they don't fit your needs, the wood-fired-oven pizzas probably will. Or the salads, sandwiches and nachos. Or the crocks of homemade soups, including such quirky Sugarloaf favorites as Cheeseburger Soup. Given Sugarloaf's close proximity to the Quebec border, The Bag even serves the French Canadian specialty *poutine*: French fries smothered in cheese and sauce. Pair your meal with a brewed-on-the-premises beer, but whatever your pleasure, get there early. The Bag's always packed for lunch and après ski, and it's jammed with families at dinner. Located in the Sugarloaf Village Center. Info: 207-237-2451 —H.N.

Gepetto's Restaurant
Carrabassett Valley, Maine

Gepetto's is a Sugarloaf institution. For more than 20 years, this casual slopeside restaurant has been serving a variety of fresh foods for lunch and dinner. Prices are reasonable, portions big and service efficient. And you can't beat the location, especially if you're popping in for a quick lunch, when an express soup-and-salad bar is offered in addition to the menu. Big windows in the plant-filled main dining room showcase the action in the village and offer a glimpse of the slopes. The menu addresses appetites both small and large. Choose from hearty soups and salads, fresh-dough pizzas, small plates such as chicken quesadilla or linguini marinara, creative pastas, or land-and-sea entrées such as lobster-stuffed haddock and barbecued baby back ribs. Nightly specials might include pistachio-encrusted rack of lamb or salmon filet. Info: 207-237-2192 —H.N.

EVENTS
The Annual Budweiser Blues Fest

Held each year in early December, this event puts big-name blues artists on center stage all weekend long. Past performers include Eddie Shaw & The Wolf Gang, Magic Slim & The Teardrops, Eddie Kirkland and Johnnie Marshall. Special ski-and-stay packages are available.

Children's Festival Week

Held in mid January, this week features nonstop kid fun such as a torch-light parade with fireworks, a kids' pajama party and parents' night out, kid pop bands in the base lodge and special races. All kids' ski-school programs are free for the week.

White, White World Week

Held the last week of January, this is when outsiders get to see what Sugarloafers are really like. Take part in zany events that include toga parties, blues night, turbo tubing, dummy jumps, snow sculpting, the crowning of Miss Sugarloaf and much more (like the cross-dressing party).

Budweiser Reggae Weekend

This is Sugarloaf's signature event. Held the first weekend of April, it's spring-skiing heaven—live reggae, lots of parties and plenty of soft snow.

INSIDER TIPS

1) Lifts without lines: To avoid the crowds at the SuperQuad, locals take the King Pine chair on the east side of the mountain, or the Bucksaw chair on the west side. Neither lift is as superfast as the SuperQuad, but lack of speed is more than offset by the absence of lines.

2) Lifts to take to follow the sun: Start in the morning at the King Pine chair on the east side, then move to the central mountain and ride the Spillway chairs (there are two side by side). From the Spillway chairs, ski down to Timberline and hit the east-facing Backside Snowfields, then circle around to the King Pine Bowl. In the afternoon, get to the West Mountain chair for some intermediate cruisers that soften up later in the day.

3) What to read to find coupons and deals: *The Original Irregular and the Seacoast.*

4) Snow stashes: For post-storm freshies, locals head to Cant Dog, Rookie River and Max Headroom. The Backside Snowfields are also awesome in the days following a storm, as prevailing winds tend to fill them back up with snow. Ripsaw, on the east side, is popular with locals for the same reason.

5) Parking secret: Shuttles pick you up at your car at every lot, so no one ever has to walk. But if you don't want to ride a shuttle, park at the base of the Snubber chair and jump on the lift, which brings you up to the base lodge and village. Ski to your car at the end of the day.

6) Finest meal for the lowest fare: Almost all of the local restaurants offer two-for-one nights. It's the best deal in town.

Sunday River
NEWRY, MAINE

SKI Magazine readers complain about getting here, eating here and partying here. So why do they come to Sunday River, and in droves? To paraphrase James Carville: It's the skiing, stupid. Sunday River consistently earns high marks for its grooming, snowmaking, and vast selection of trails. What leads one *SKI* reader to grouse "nothing there but skiing" is probably the same thing that inspires others to say "best area in the East" and "about as good as it gets." True, there isn't much of an après scene (though the recent addition of a free trolley service brought thousands of skiers to Bethel's Norman Rockwell-style downtown, improving the much-maligned shopping and dining options) and the condos aren't much to look at. But snap on the skis and you're bound to smile. Chances are good that compared to most other Eastern resorts the trails will be whiter and better corduroyed, the lifts so myriad and fast that even on holiday weekends lift lines will be nil. And those 128 trails, from the killer bumps of Agony to the mellow curves of Lollapalooza, provide enough space and variety for entire families to disappear for days. The *SKI* reader who describes the off-mountain experience as "generally not up to what it takes to attract a national following" is right. But so is the one who says, "most consistent ski experience in the East."

VITAL STATS

SUMMIT: 3,140 feet

VERTICAL DROP: 2,340 feet

SKIABLE ACRES: 663

BEGINNER: 25%

INTERMEDIATE: 35%

ADVANCED/EXPERT: 40%

SNOWMAKING: 92% coverage

AVG. ANNUAL SNOWFALL: 155 in.

LIFTS: 18; 4 high-speed quads, 5 fixed quads, 4 triples, 2 doubles, 3 surface lifts

TERRAIN PARKS/HALFPIPES: 4 terrain parks, 2 halfpipes

INFO: 800-543-2SKI; www.sundayriver.com

Sunday River offers four terrain parks, a superpipe and a quarterpipe.

SKIING IT

Saturday morning we picked up our gear at the outdoor ski check and skied down to the Jordan Bowl Express Quad. Jordan is the western-most of Sunday River's eight peaks, but friends had warned us that it draws a crowd. So we got there before anyone else and swooped down Rogue Angel, warming our muscles as we caught air over its many rollers. While most of Sunday River's trails are of newer design—wide and mostly straight down the fall line—manmade terrain features enliven the experience, as do glades and terrain parks, of which Sunday River has many.

From the summit of Jordan, we headed east on Kansas, which delivered us through the Oz and Aurora Peak areas to North Peak. North Peak is the resort's heart, the point from which human traffic pulses east, west, up, and down as it moves to Sunday River's extremities. The South Ridge complex at North Peak's base is the resort's main facility, and after one run, we knew this was an area to avoid. One oasis worth finding amid the madness, however, was the Perfect Turn Express Quad, a.k.a. Lift 6, where lift lines seldom accumulate. We cruised Escapade and Dream Maker, loosened our knees on 3D, an intermediate bump run, then took the plunge on double-black Northern Exposure.

After refueling at the North Peak Lodge, we considered a run off Spruce Peak, but our timing was bad. American Express, Risky Business and Downdraft, long fall-line trails all, are three of the most popular runs at the resort. We should have skied there earlier in the morning, when the snow was fresh and the skiers few. Instead, we slid over to Barker Mountain.

Barker and Locke Mountains provide some of Sunday River's best advanced terrain. As we rode Lift 1, the Sunday River Express Quad, to Barker's summit, we eyed Agony, an appropriately named bump run, but opted for Right Stuff, a playful plunge that invited long, carved GS turns. Next, we cut over to Locke on Jungle Road and descended T2, thrilling with each pop off the undulating terrain before hanging a right over to White Cap.

White Cap is home to Sunday River's most notorious trail, White Heat; it's the "longest, steepest, widest" trail in the East, the resort boasts. This trail, like a tragicomic mask, is divided in half vertically: One side meticulously groomed, the other mega-bumped. Serious skiers who don't need audience feedback from the chairlift head to the double-black Chutzpah and Hard Ball glades, which flank White Heat and add trees to the mix of bumps and steeps. On a local's advice, we sought out Shock Wave, which has nearly the pitch of White Heat, but doesn't attract the crowds. It was good advice.

Purposefully, we saved the best terrain for last. Oz and Aurora are laced with black and double-black terrain, yet are the least-crowded peaks at the resort. No high-speed quads here. No base lodges, either. Most skiers and riders pass through on their way from one peak to the other, which is just fine with the regulars, who are happy to have the double-black Celestial and Flying Monkey glades to themselves. —H.N.

FAMILY MATTERS

Like all American Skiing Company resorts, Sunday River offers the Perfect Kids Program, which ranges from daycare for tiny tots to starter programs for toddlers to challenging programs for young bucks ready to tear up the mountain. The daycare services children ages six weeks to six years.

Sunday River's three sites for kids' lessons—the South Ridge Base Lodge, the Jordan Grand Resort Hotel, and the Grand Summit Resort Hotel—are spread nicely across the resort, which is all but essential for a ski area that ranges so wide. And Sunday River's breadth is something that parents should be mindful of: Establishing clear meeting points and times for the kids will assure that they don't end up three peaks away come lunch time.

When not skiing, families can find a lot to do at the White Cap Fun Center. Located on-mountain and accessible by a complimentary trolley service, the Center offers a lighted ice skating rink, an arcade, a lighted tubing park and family dining. If mom and dad aren't up to frolicking in the snow, they can eat dinner while the kids have fun right outside the door.

MAINE

GETTING THERE
From Portland

Take the Maine Turnpike (I-495) North to Exit 11. Take Route 26 North to Route 2 East and take a left onto Sunday River Road. Follow signs to resort.

Drive Time: 1.5 hours

From Boston

Take I-95 North to the Maine Turnpike (I-495). Take I-495 North to Exit 11. Take Route 26 North to Route 2 East and take a left onto Sunday River Road. Follow signs to resort.

Drive Time: 3 hours

From New York City

Take I-84 east to the Massachusetts Turnpike (I-90). Take I-90 East to Exit 10. Take Route 290 North to Route 495 North to I-95. Take I-95 North to the Maine Turnpike (I-495) North to Exit 11. Take Route 26 North Route 2 East and take a left onto Sunday River Road. Follow signs to resort.

Drive Time: 7 hours

LODGING

On-mountain lodging is almost the only game in town, but there are some options away from the slopes. For the following slopeside accommodations, book through the Sunday River's central reservations (800-543-2SKI).

The Grand Summit Resort Hotel

The flagship of all American Skiing Company Resorts, the Grand Summit offers the most amenities available slopeside. At Sunday River, these include two restaurants, a health club, a heated outdoor pool, valet parking, daycare, ski check, a game room and concierge service. Accommodations range from standard hotel rooms to one-bedroom suites with kitchenettes. You can't beat the ski-in–ski-out convenience, but some of the rooms have the thinnest walls in ski country.

The Jordan Grand Resort Hotel

Sunday River's newest slopeside hotel is located smack in the middle of the Jordan Bowl area and offers many of the same amenities as the Grand Summit, including restaurants, an outdoor heated pool, health

There are over 700 slope-side condominium units spread across the resort.

club, spa, valet parking, ski check and more. The difference is living space—here you can get anything from a standard room to a two-bedroom suite with a kitchen.

Snow Cap Inn

Understated, relaxed, and not overly opulent, the Snow Cap offers an affordable alternative without sacrificing easy access to the slopes. Each room has two queen-size beds and a private bath. Amenities include two fireside lounges, ski lockers, a fitness room and an outdoor hot tub.

Sunday River Condos

Sunday River has over 700 condominium units spread across the resort—all slopeside with direct access to the trails. Sizes range from studio units to three-bedroom townhouses, and all include kitchens, access to indoor or outdoor pools, and a host of other amenities. Most have their own heated outdoor pools, and those that don't have direct access to one in a complex next door.

Bethel Inn & Country Club
Bethel, Maine

Long before Sunday River emerged as a major resort, the Bethel Inn was a compelling destination in its own right. Built in 1913 by a physician and his appreciative patients, this grand country spa proved so effective in soothing (and detoxing) overstressed academics that it came to be called "the resting place of Harvard." Nowadays, guests tend to indulge in the very pursuits that put the profs over the top. The hotel's distinguished New American restaurant has a wine cellar to match, so the chef can recommend delectable pairings such as cedar-planked salmon with a 1995 Pouilly-Fuissé. Common rooms—including a study lined with Charles Dana Gibson drawings—are as grand as the restaurant's glass veranda. Forty kilometers of cross-country trails fan out across the snowed-under 200-acre golf course, and Sunday River is a free, 10-minute shuttle ride away. The inn recently added 16 new rooms, eight with Jacuzzis. It also has contemporary spa facilities, which include a steaming outdoor pool and hot tub. Lift-and-lodging packages are reasonably priced. Info: 800-654-0125; www.bethelinn.com —S.M.

Briar Lea Inn and Restaurant
Bethel, Maine

The Briar Lea strikes the perfect balance between fancy inn and B&B. The 150-year-old Georgian farmhouse, just outside Bethel village, has six guestrooms, including a two-room suite that's ideal for families. All the rooms are nicely, but not fussily, decorated; all have private baths and TVs. What sets the Briar Lea apart is its restaurant: excellent food, fair prices, comfortable setting. It's fancy enough for table clothes, casual enough to have a children's menu. Entrées include Medi spaghetti, rainbow trout, roast duck and filet mignon. The dining room is also open to the public for breakfast; specialties include Belgian waffles, French toast and moose-biscuit Benedict, a variation on the classic. Info: 877-311-1299; www.briarleainnrestaurant.com —H.N.

The Victoria Inn
Bethel, Maine

This three-story, Queen Anne–style inn and restaurant on Bethel's Main Street is painted in shades of beige, mauve and teal, and adorned with a copper-roofed turret. The attached carriage house, topped with a glass-paned cupola, dwarfs the house. Inside, oak woodwork, ceiling rosettes and antique furnishings capture the era's elegance without its stuffiness. Guest rooms in the main house are perfect for couples seeking a romantic retreat, while the two-bedroom units in the carriage house are ideal for families. Rates run the gamut, and breakfast is included. The Carriage House also has a private living room, where guests can relax away from

MAINE

the dinner crowd. Dinner is open to the public by reservation and is reason enough for a visit. Soft music and lighting, rich linens, and lovely china and crystal create an appropriate ambiance for Chef Eric Botka's fine cuisine, which might include tenderloin au poivre, rack of lamb, or duck Victoria. For dessert, the crème brulée is exquisite. Info: 207-824-8060, 888-774-1235; www.victoria-inn.com

The Lake House
Waterford, Maine

Just 25 minutes from Sunday River in sleepy Waterford, check out the circa-1797 Lake House where chef-owner Michael Myers serves delectable roast duckling and filet mignon in his charming eight-room inn. Call in advance, book a room, and stay for the night. The price for two, including breakfast, is one of the most charming deals around. Info: 800-223-4182

DINING
Mother's
Bethel, Maine

Over the Androscoggin River and through the woods of White Mountain National Forest to Mother's house you should go. At first glance, the gingerbread-trimmed, light-green farmhouse six miles from Sunday River doesn't appear to be a restaurant. Don't be fooled. Inside are three cozy dining rooms and an enclosed porch. Deep burgundy walls, wood floors, and, as one staff member puts it, "books, nooks and woodstoves," create a warm, homey atmosphere. Equally warming are Mother's hearty pastas, soups, stews and popular cheese fondue for two. With a name like Mother's, you might expect meat loaf and fried chicken. Not here, where fresh seafood is a specialty—don't miss the crab cakes. Salads, steaks, lamb and duck are also on the menu. And bring the kids: Mother's has a great children's menu. Info: 207-824-2589 —H.N.

Sunday River Brewing Company
Bethel, Maine

In its fifth season on the banks of the Androscoggin River and in the shadow of Mount Will, this beer haven is three miles from the slopes and a pillar of the Sunday River après-ski scene. And when spring finally rolls around, which is late in Maine, the SRBC is as prepared as a Boy Scout.

Snow is sculpted into "keg refrigerators" on the flagstone patio, a sand volleyball court is installed, and picnic tables are set up. There are even Adirondack patio chairs with wide arms designed to coddle a tipsy pitcher of beer. Kick off the afternoon with a six-brew sampler paddle. Then again, you could move right into the big leagues with a pint of Black Bear Porter (aggressively hopped) or Sunday River Alt (balanced and well-rounded). The Brew Co. also serves up a full menu of American pub fare. Info: 207-824-4253

EVENTS
The Annual Santa Sunday and Santa Weekend

The first weekend of December, Sunday River offers a free lift ticket for anyone who shows up dressed as Santa and donates a holiday gift to needy children. In past years, hundreds of Santas have schussed.

Maine Handicap Ski-a-Thon

A life-changing program that serves hundreds of people with disabilities and is the largest single-day fundraiser in the state of Maine. Held in mid March.

Annual Bust 'n' Burn Mogul Competition and Parrot Head Festival

New England's top amateur and pro bump skiers compete on White Heat. The event also includes pond skimming, live music, parties and more.

INSIDER TIPS
1) Lifts without lines: North Peak (Lift 6) and Aurora (Lift 12), and also Locke Mountain (Lift 4) and Oz (Lift 15), which are generally open weekends only.

2) Lifts to take to follow the sun: Start in the morning at Spruce Peak (Lift 8) and make your way to White Cap (Lift 10). From there, make your way back to the other side of the mountain toward Jordan Bowl (Lift 14).

3) What to read to find coupons and deals: Pick up the *Bethel Citizen* to find a comprehensive calendar of events, or *Sunday River This Week*, the on-mountain publication with ads from local businesses.

4) Snow stashes: On the map it's Bim's Whim off Locke and Celestial off Aurora. Off the map try between Bim's Whim and T2 (but you didn't hear it from us).

5) Parking secret: White Cap Base Lodge.

6) Finest meal for the lowest fare: Sud's Pub, located in the basement of the Sudbury Inn on Main Street in Bethel, is great for casual dining. Upstairs, the dining room has finer selections and often offers fixed-price wine-tasting dinners and other specials.

THE BEST OF THE REST OF MAINE

Saddleback Ski Area

RANGELEY, MAINE

We were halfway up the double chair at Saddleback when my friend Scott said, "So. Seen anyone yet?" It was a Wednesday in early March, plenty of snow, a great day to ski—and for some strange reason the employees outnumbered the paying customers. We wouldn't see more than 10 skiers the entire day.

Why? Good question. Saddleback has about as much actual vertical descent as Sunday River, and its summit elevation of 4,120 feet makes it the second-highest ski mountain in Maine (behind Sugarloaf) and one of the 10 highest in New England. The summit has a wilderness feel—lift-served backcountry, stunted spruces encased in hoar frost, and views of the famous Rangeley Lakes area. The mountain's got a good mix of trails, from wide, gentle cruisers such as Haymaker to the narrow, plunging Muleskinner, which rivals anything at Vermont's famously challenging Mad River Glen. It's a friendly, laid-back, family-oriented place in one of Maine's greatest outdoor regions. And you sure as hell don't have to worry about lift lines. Even on the weekends, 300 is considered a crowd.

VITAL STATS

SUMMIT: 4,120 feet
VERTICAL DROP: 1,830 feet
SKIABLE ACRES: 100
BEGINNER: 34%
INTERMEDIATE: 33%
ADVANCED/EXPERT: 33%
SNOWMAKING: 50% coverage
AVG. ANNUAL SNOWFALL: 200 in.
LIFTS: 5; 2 doubles and 3 T-bars
TERRAIN PARKS/HALFPIPES:
  1 terrain park, no halfpipes
INFO: 207-864-5671;
  www.saddlebackskiarea.com

So, again, why? Well, the place isn't perfect. Whoever changed the names of the runs from fly-fishing classics like Grey Ghost to Wild West themes such as El Hombre and Cowpoke's Cruise deserves to be exiled to Texas. More important, as one local said, "it's 1970s skiing." You ride a poky double chair and a T-bar to access the peak, and the snowmaking won't win any awards.

Moreover, Saddleback suffers from benign neglect. That's because it's located in one of Maine's unorganized territories (as opposed to a settled town), which means it needs permission from a state commission for trail cutting and improvements.

Now, owner Donald Breen, a Massachusetts pharmaceutical manufacturer who bought the area 25 years ago, is retiring from the ski industry and selling the resort. It is listed with Sotheby's International Realty and has garnered quite a bit of interest from potential buyers. However, if the 8,000-acre property does not sell, Saddleback may not open for the upcoming season. Play it safe and call before you leave. Or, if you have $7.5 million lying around, call Sotheby's and make them an offer—pure skiing mountains like this don't come along everyday. —N.R.

GETTING THERE

From Portland
Take the Maine Turnpike (I-495) to Exit 31. Take Route 27 North to Route 4 North to Rangeley and Saddleback.

Drive Time: 2.5 hours

From Boston
Take I-95 North to the Maine Turnpike (I-495) to Exit 12. Take Route 4 North to Rangeley and Saddleback.

Drive Time: 4.5 hours

DINING

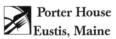

Porter House
Eustis, Maine

You just don't expect to find a restaurant like the Porter House in a place like Eustis—a tiny town better known for good fishing and hunting than fine dining. But the Porter House is considered one of the region's best restaurants, worth the drive from Saddleback or Sugarloaf. Folks even come from Canada for the quiet ambiance, good continental fare (duck is a house specialty) and savvy wine list. The restaurant is located in an old New England farmhouse, and though white tablecloths and candles set a mood, the restaurant is popular with families, too. The wide-ranging menu includes such items as a vegetarian Portofino Pie with artichoke hearts, spinach, and ricotta baked in a puff pastry; porterhouse steak; Lobster Brittany Casserole with mushrooms and sherry; and Chicken Fromage baked with cheddar and herb cheeses. The bread and salad dressings are made on premises, as are the desserts. And no self-respecting chocoholic should miss the Chocolate Pot, a fudgey, moussey concoction topped with sweet whipped cream. In any case, make reservations in advance. This may be the boonies, but it's almost always a full house. Info: 207-246-7932

Big Squaw Mountain Resort
GREENVILLE, MAINE

My first few years of skiing in Maine were spent at the usual high-profile resorts, cruising the wide-open intermediates at Sunday River or testing my nerves and technique on the upper reaches of Sugarloaf.

All the while, though, friends were raving about an out-of-the-way treasure called Big Squaw Mountain Resort, a mid-sized area located near Moosehead Lake in the remote northern part of the state. "The views!" they'd gush. "The snow!" One realist, after enthusing about the vistas and powder, added, "I damn near froze my face off."

When I could stand it no longer, I packed the car and headed for Greenville, a humble dot of civilization minutes from Big Squaw. For all its remoteness, Greenville is a mere three hours from my home in Portland—a bit far-flung for a same-day outing, perhaps, but not an epic road trip, either.

VITAL STATS

SUMMIT: 3,200 feet

VERTICAL DROP: 1,750 feet

SKIABLE ACRES: 400

BEGINNER: 33%

INTERMEDIATE: 34%

ADVANCED/EXPERT: 33%

SNOWMAKING: 70% coverage

AVG. ANNUAL SNOWFALL: 150 in.

LIFTS: 3; 1 triple, 1 double, 1 T-bar and 1 pony lift

TERRAIN PARKS/HALFPIPES: 1 terrain park, 1 halfpipe

INFO: 207-695-1000; www.bigsquawmountain.com

Once on Big Squaw's slopes, I realized what all the gushing was about: good base, plenty of natural fluffy stuff, short lift lines, great views and 1,750 vertical feet of challenging terrain. Did I mention great views? Off the

Sights from Big Squaw include Moosehead Lake, Mount Kineo and Mount Katahdin.

Penobscot Trail, a 2.5-mile intermediate cruiser, I could look out over the entirety of the 40-mile-long Moosehead Lake, past the distinctive jut of 1,800-foot Mt. Kineo at the lake's narrows, to 5,240-foot Mt. Katahdin in the distance. On my first trip down Penobscot, I risked face-planting with all my rubbernecking, so I finally pulled over at a break in the birches and took it all in. The cost of those great views was skiing into the teeth of a steady north wind. I didn't quite freeze my face off, but by the end of each run I was already dreading the chilly lift ride back up.

Big Squaw has been around since 1963 and has been owned by Scott Paper Co., the state, and various private interests (currently a Florida businessman), but it hasn't changed much since its earliest days. There's a triple chair and 70 percent snowmaking coverage; various upgrades, such as a pool and saunas, are being added to the base hotel. But the place has a determinedly retro feel that's refreshing in this age of ski-area-as-entertainment-complex. It's out of the way enough to escape the hordes that clog most Northeast resorts every weekend, but how long it can retain its quirky local character while remaining viable is anybody's guess.

In the meantime, I'm spreading the Big Squaw gospel to my friends. The snow! The views! Only next time, I tell them, I'm wearing heavier base layers. —S.S.

GETTING THERE
From Portland

Take I-95 North to Newport exit. Take Route 7/11 to Dexter. Take Route 23 to Guilford and Route 15 to Big Squaw Mountain.

Drive Time: 3 hours

From Quebec City

Take Canada Route 173 to Jackman, Maine. Take Route 6/15 to Big Squaw Mountain.

Drive Time: 3 hours

LODGING

The resort includes a 56-room hotel, with dining rooms, lounge, base lodge, ski school, and ski shop.

Inn At Moosehead Lake
Greenville, Maine

After a day on the slopes at Squaw, the Inn at Moosehead Lake is a welcoming retreat. Innkeepers Roger and Jennifer Cauchi have built a reputation for offering big city–style service and amenities in a small inn on the edge of the Great North Woods. From its hillside setting, the inn commands sweeping views of Moosehead Lake and the snow-covered wilderness, and Jennifer's painstaking decor succeeds at bringing the outside in. Ivory walls and carpeting are warmed with soothing earth-toned fabrics, Asian rugs and artfully placed natural accents, such as branches and twigs, pine cones—even small evergreens. The eight spacious guest rooms have gas fireplaces, Jacuzzi tubs, TV/VCRs, hand-carved four-poster beds and comfortable sitting areas, not to mention such niceties as fresh fruit, full ice buckets, hair dryers and coffee makers. It's tempting to wile away the day by the fieldstone fireplace in the Great Room, but you also might want to get some exercise between the leisurely, multi-course gourmet breakfasts and dinners. In the evening, retreat to the game room for billiards and darts, or to your own room for a quiet evening with a selection from the extensive video library. Info: 207-695-4400, www.lodgeatmooseheadlake.com —H.N.

Shawnee Peak

BRIDGTON, MAINE

When my parents took back my childhood room, I barely noticed. When they sold the house, I didn't bat an eye. But when they sold our camp at Shawnee Peak, I cried.

Shawnee, formerly Pleasant Mountain, is a mid-size area less than an hour from Portland, Maine, and 30 minutes from North Conway, New Hampshire. Like thousands of other kids from greater Portland, I progressed from wedge to parallel on Shawnee's slopes, soaked up spring rays on its decks, and imitated the distinctive ski style of the cool kids (elbows in, turns initiated at the shoulders—to this day, the dead giveaway of an early '70s Pleasant Mountain skier).

The mountain rises out of Moose Pond in the middle of nowhere, with views of Mt. Washington and the Presidentials to the west. But don't be deceived by the rural setting: Shawnee is the largest night-skiing slope in New England, and it hums, day and night.

Families from Maine, New Hampshire and Massachusetts are drawn here by equal parts low-key atmosphere and decent skiing. The mountain's 1,300-foot vertical is laced with predominantly intermediate runs on two faces—a mixture of wide slopes and winding trails with just enough steeps and moguls to keep you interested. Beginners get their own segregated area. Trails such as Jack Spratt, Haggett's Hurdle, Cody's Caper, Peter's Plunge and Riley's Run are as fun to ski as they are to say. The trails on the main face appear to spell out "lov" in '60s-style block letters, especially when viewed at night.

Shawnee has a rich history. It opened in 1938 and went on to boast Maine's first T-bar (1955) and first chairlift (1963). In the early '70s, its ski school director, former Swiss National Team member Ruedi Wyrsch, put Shawnee at the forefront of the emerging freestyle and ballet movement. Wyrsch was renowned for his tip stands and stilt skiing, and he and fellow coach Bruce "Boogie" Boyle nurtured some of the earliest

VITAL STATS

SUMMIT: 1,900 feet
VERTICAL DROP: 1,300 feet
SKIABLE ACRES: 239
BEGINNER: 25%
INTERMEDIATE: 50%
ADVANCED/EXPERT: 25%
SNOWMAKING: 98% coverage
AVG. ANNUAL SNOWFALL: 105 in.
LIFTS: 5; 1 quad, 2 triples, 1 double, 1 surface lift
TERRAIN PARKS/HALFPIPES: 1 terrain park, 1 halfpipe
INFO: 207-647-8444; www.shawneepeak.com

Shawnee Peak is a family-friendly mountain with wide slopes, winding trails and a separate beginner's area.

talents of the discipline, including filmmaker Greg Stump and his brother Geoff, Frank Howell, Peter Young, Doug Rand and Canadian Olympian Leelee Morrison.

Shawnee just turned 65. Despite bad winters, near bankruptcies, and changes in ownership and name during the '80s and early '90s, the area survives. Under current ownership, it's again thriving—and again capturing the hearts of families like mine. —H.N.

GETTING THERE
From Portland
Take Route 302 West past Bridgeton. Turn left on Mountain Road to Shawnee Peak.

Drive Time: 1 hour

From Portsmouth
Take I-95 North to Exit 8 on Maine Turnpike (I-495). Take Route 302 West past Bridgton. Turn left on Mountain Road to Shawnee Peak.

Drive Time: 1. 5 hours

From Boston
Take I-93 North to I-95. Take I-95 North to Exit 8 on Maine Turnpike (I-495). Take Route 302 West past Bridgton. Turn left on Mountain Road to Shawnee Peak.

Drive Time: 2.5 hours

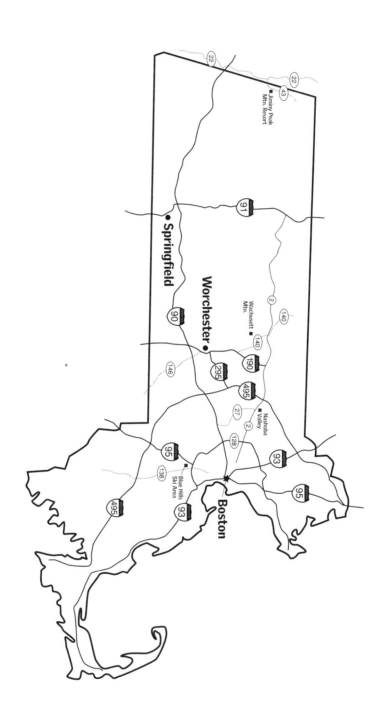

Massachusetts

SKI MAGAZINE'S GUIDE TO NEW ENGLAND AND QUEBEC

Jiminy Peak Mountain Resort

HANCOCK, MASSACHUSETTS

Tens of thousands of people vacation each year in what they think are the Berkshire Mountains. Those people are mistaken. There's no such place as the Berkshire Mountains. Technically, according to Webster's New World Dictionary, the Berkshires are a "region of wooded hills in Western Massachusetts." Mountains, no. Hills, yes. So, while the heavily forested terrain is as beautiful and unspoiled as just about any in New England, the Berkshires are decidedly more round than steep. And for skiers, that means the majority of the Berkshires have "intermediate" stamped all over them. Jiminy Peak, however, is a surprising exception. The 55-year-old area, the largest in the Bay State, has 1,150 vertical feet and several trails steep and long enough to keep strong intermediates puffing and experts itching for another run. Three gladed areas were recently thinned out of the forest to beef up the resort's challenge. The charming ski area still has much of its "good old days" appeal. It traces its history to 1943, when Berkshire ski pioneer Bart Hendricks purchased 300 acres of mountain property for less than two bucks an acre. After an opening delayed by World War II, the ski area debuted in December of 1948 with five trails and a $3 lift ticket. —B.R.

VITAL STATS

SUMMIT: 2,380 feet

VERTICAL DROP: 1,150 feet

SKIABLE ACRES: 156

BEGINNER: 10%

INTERMEDIATE: 43%

ADVANCED/EXPERT: 47%

SNOWMAKING: 93% coverage

AVG. ANNUAL SNOWFALL: 100 in.

LIFTS: 8; Berkshire Express Six, 2 high-speed quads, 3 triples, 1 double, 1 surface lifts

TERRAIN PARKS/HALFPIPES: 1 terrain park, 1 halfpipe

INFO: 413-738-5500; www.jiminypeak.com

SKIING IT

Jiminy's "peak" is actually a broad, flat summit with three lifts strung across it. The Triple chair, which starts near the on-slope Country Inn at the base, gets you to the west side of the mountaintop. The Exhibition Chair, a double situated near the Crane day lodge, runs to the center of the summit. You can also reach the top by riding the short Novice chair next to Exhibition and then skiing down to Jiminy's Q1 quad, which takes you to the east side of the mountaintop. The top stations of all three lifts unload onto a broad, flat staging area, which requires some skating and poling to get around.

A good way for advanced skiers to warm up and become familiar with Jiminy's terrain is to take the Triple chair to the summit when the lifts open at 8:30 A.M. Start by skiing West Way, an easier intermediate trail that leads to Grand Slam, which is similarly pitched. Save the trails that break off to the right of West Way for later in the day. Instead, ski to the bottom of Grand Slam and bear right to the Exhibition chair. At the top, head left for a long warm-up run down the two-mile Left Bank. If the Exhibition lift line is too long, ride the Novice chair and transfer to the Q1 quad for your second ride to the top.

Better skiers may want to pass on the second warm-up run after seeing Whitetail, which runs beneath Q1. In a bit of creative marketing, Jiminy claims Whitetail is "New England's steepest, longest black-diamond lighted run." Take away the lights and Whitetail is a doe to Stowe's Nose Dive buck, but it is one of the three trails that put Jiminy in the ballpark for skiers craving steep pitches.

On either side of Exhibition are the two other reasons why strong skiers stopped turning their noses up at Jiminy several seasons ago: Jericho to skier's left and Upper Whirlaway to skier's right. Jericho is Jiminy's toughest run and is often sprinkled with big bumps.

Don't be confused by the name changes you see on the trail map. Upper Whirlaway becomes Exhibition East on the lower half, but the two are really a single connected trail from the top of the quad to the bottom. The best skiers on the hill are here, and some spend the entire day just yo-yoing the quad.

When it's time for a change of pace, check out the trails that drop off to the right of West Way. The first two, North Glade and Lower Glade, are misnamed. They may have started out as glades, but are now wide, tree-less runs with decent pitch. Both trails lead to the easier Upper Slingshot, which in turn leads to a trail fork. From the fork, take Lower Slingshot back to the bottom of the Triple chair. If you pass on the North and Lower Glades cutoffs on West Way, you'll come to the Jiminy's new glades—Riptide and Willie's Gulch. They're not exceptionally long, but they are true glades in the New England tradition.

For rank beginners, the resort's Cricket Triple chairlift serves lots of novice terrain and is ideal for never-evers. Set apart from the main slopes and trails, Jiminy's gentle beginner slopes have no surprise dips or bumps,

Jiminy Peak traces its history to 1943, when Berkshire ski pioneer Bart Hendricks purchased 300 acres of mountain property for less than $2 per acre.

and no cross-traffic from better skiers. The Novice chair, on the bottom of the main mountain, services slightly steeper—but still very easy—terrain. The two combine to make for a perfect progression for skiers just starting out.

Snowboarders and new-school skiers will be drawn to the Grand Slam chair near the Country Inn. Grand Slam services Jiminy's Alpine Terrain Park, an area with bumps, rails, various hits and a quarterpipe. —B.R.

FAMILY MATTERS

Perhaps the most pro-family thing you can say about Jiminy is that it's precisely the type of place at which families have been learning to ski together since the sport's been around: Not too big, not too expensive, not too far away, not too intimidating. And even if you're only a couple of hours away, Jiminy's slopeside lodging—yes, it's got some—can allow for a very manageable, smaller-scale weekend getaway that is a great first step before hauling the kids off to someplace like Stowe or the big mountains out West.

For parents who want to put their children into a program, the Burbank Children's Center accommodates up to 350 children. SKIwee is for kids four to eight years old; Jiminy's Explorers is for skiers from nine to 12; Mountain Adventures caters to strong skiers six to 17 years old. Children 6 months and older who prefer indoor play can spend time in the new playroom. It can accommodate an additional 42 children and reservations are required.

GETTING THERE
From Albany

Take I-90 East to Exit 8 to Route 43 East. Turn Right on Brodie Mountain Road and watch for Jiminy peak on right.

Drive Time: 1 hour

From Boston

Take the Massachusetts Turnpike (I-90) West to Exit B-3 (Berkshire Spur section). Take Route 22 North to Route 43 East. Turn Right on Brodie Mountain Road and watch for Jiminy peak on right.

Drive Time: 3 hours

From New York City

Take the Taconic Parkway North to Route 295 East, to Route 22 North to Route 43 East. Turn Right on Brodie Mountain Road and watch for Jiminy Peak on right.

Drive Time: 3 hours

LODGING
Slopeside and Village Lodging

Situated at the base of the mountain, the Country Inn is an honest-to-goodness slopeside lodge at Jiminy Peak. It may seem strange that what seems to most folks like a day ski area has slopeside accommodations, but you can have a near-Vermontlike experience here without investing as much time on the road—and you won't regret it. A one-bedroom hotel suite (with a pullout queen sofa in the living room) with lift tickets is very reasonably priced. A little farther away, two- and three-bedroom condos are available at Country Village, which is an easy walk to Jiminy's Village Center. Booking for both options is handled by Jiminy's central reservations. Info: 800-882-8859

The Little Farm B&B
Hancock, Massachusetts

A working farm with barns and live animals, the Little Farm is located just minutes from the resort. The recently enlarged house dates to the early 1940s, but it looks older. Three rooms share a common bath; one room and a single suite have private baths. Guests can snowshoe and cross-country ski on 30 acres of fields and woods. The rates are a bargain. Info: 413-458-5492

The Orchards
Williamstown, Massachusetts

The Orchards is the state's only Mobil Four Star and AAA Four Diamond rated hotel outside of Boston. Set in the classic New England college town of Williamstown, staying here gives you a lot of dining and entertainment options nearby and an authentic New England university-town vibe. Decorated with English antiques and oriental accent pieces, the Orchards has 65 silver teapots and makes good use of them during afternoon tea. Info: 413-458-9611

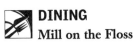 **DINING**
Mill on the Floss
Lanesboro, Massachusetts

The area's best restaurant is the rustic but upscale Mill on the Floss. Chef and owner Maurice Champagne works culinary magic in a display kitchen rimmed with copper pots and pans. You can't go wrong with the crab cakes with Dijon sauce or the sliced tenderloin with garlic sauce. Rack of lamb is the priciest entrée. Info: 413-458-9123

Hobson's Choice
Williamstown, Massachusetts

It doesn't look like much from the outside, but Hobson's, located on Water Street, is famous for its blackened meat, chicken and fish dishes. Info: 413-458-9101

INSIDER TIPS

1) Lifts without lines: The Berkshire Express is always the best way to the top. Lift lines even on the busiest days are never more than five minutes. Once you are at the top, Widow White's quad is the best ride on the mountain. Never a lift line, and it's the only way to access the upper 75% of four of the trails on Widow White's Peak, which means lots of room for turns.

2) What lifts to take to follow the sun: Start on the Summit triple, and then move to Widow White's quad.

3) Newspapers and local magazines to read to find coupons and deals: *The Entertainment Card* has a two-for-one coupon.

4) Snow stashes: Willie's Gulch and Riptide for tree skiing.

5) Parking secret: Park behind the mountain-operations building, among the bulldozers and old snowcats. You'll walk about 20 steps to the beginner slope and can catch that chair to reach the others that serve more advanced terrain.

6) Finest meal for the lowest fare: Powderhounds, at the entrance to Jiminy Peak, or The Old Forge on Route 7 in Lanesboro, about 10 minutes away.

Wachusett Mountain

PRINCETON, MASSACHUSETTS

Though it has only 18 trails and five lifts, Wachusett, with 325,000 skier visits every year, is among New England's five most popular ski resorts. It gets more visitors than Waterville Valley and Wildcat, New Hampshire, and more than even Stratton, Vermont. But with the exception of Sundays with good weather, which resemble midsummer days at Jones Beach, it never seems to get too crowded here. How does Wachusett do it? Simple: It remakes itself every three hours. Open from 9 A.M. (8 A.M. on weekends) to 10 P.M., Wachusett changes its customer demographics four times each weekday. You can set your clock by it: Every three hours, a new and completely different group of skiers—from old-timers to head-bangers—arrives to take the place of the group that came before. The transitions are seamless thanks to Wachusett's army of employees and slew of on-snow programs. Each successive wave of skiers arrives, piles into the sleek, 28,000-square-foot day lodge, loads onto the high-speed quad, and spills out onto slopes covered top to bottom by a multimillion-dollar snowmaking system.

VITAL STATS

SUMMIT: 2,006 feet

VERTICAL DROP: 1,000 feet

SKIABLE ACRES: 105

BEGINNER: 30%

INTERMEDIATE: 40%

ADVANCED/EXPERT: 30%

SNOWMAKING: 100% coverage

AVG. ANNUAL SNOWFALL: 100 in.

LIFTS: 5; 2 high-speed quads, 1 triple, 2 surface lifts

TERRAIN PARKS/HALFPIPES: 1 terrain park, 1 halfpipe

INFO: 978-464-2300; www.wachusett.com

All of Wachusett's trails and lifts are lit for night skiing.

SKIING IT

Wachusett makes anyone's skiing day simple with its no-nonsense layout. The resort's three main lifts, all easily accessible by foot from the base area, each cater to a different level of skier. Beginners head straight to the Monadock chair, where they find all kinds of short and longer trails to explore. The chair also empties down into the Polar Playground, where smaller children, beginners or not, like to hang out. Intermediates will find gentle pitches and a bit of challenge off the Minuteman Express. The terrain park and halfpipe are also accessed by the Minuteman, which makes it a good lift for parents and their thrill-seeking teenagers to spend time on together. Advanced skiers beeline it to the Polar Express, which takes them up top to the more advanced terrain. There, lovers of challenge can try their hand at the 10th Mountain Trail or the roller-coaster fun of Conifer Connection, where heart-pounding pitches are interspersed with gentle bailouts for those who need to catch their breath.

Wachusett's compartmentalized setup is nice. Most skiers choose their level of challenge and stick to that part of the mountain. It keeps beginners on gentle terrain, away from places they might get nervous (or get in the way), and it keeps the real screamers in a zone where they won't scare the more conservative skier. If you happen to end up at a section you don't like, don't fret. The aptly named Mass Pike catwalk cuts across the mountain and can easily get you to anywhere you want to be.

Wachusett has night skiing, too. Unlike other resorts that light up a trail or two and call themselves open, Wachusett does it right. Every single trail and lift open during the daytime is also open at night.

FAMILY MATTERS

Wachusett folks like to say that it takes a "friendly family" to make a mountain family friendly. The Crowleys, who own and operate Wachusett and raised their kids here, saw firsthand the good and bad of family skiing as their children grew. They adapted their programs from what they learned. The result is obvious from the moment you pull in, when the Wachusett "Fun Patrol" approaches your car and offers to load your gear into a sled and pull it to the base area. Then there's the learning area and its "ski carousel," which pulls kids around a realistic-looking carousel to teach them the feeling of skis moving on snow. There are also all the usual ski programs for all ages, a nursery for those too young to ski, and a racer/freestyle development program for those ready to do something more with their skiing.

Wachusett has some truly unique offerings, too. Programs such as "Science on the Mountain," which teaches kids about everything from ecology to snowmaking, are run throughout the season. Kids can have fun, learn something and even go back to school with a paper topic. Imagine that.

GETTING THERE
From Boston

Take Route 2 West to Exit 25. Take Route 140 South to access road and Wachusett Mountain.

Drive Time: 1 hour

From Providence

Take Route 146 North to I-290 East to I-190 North to Exit 5. Take Route 140 North to access road and Wachusett Mountain.

Drive Time: 1.5 hours

From Hartford

Take Route 84 East to the Massachusetts Turnpike (I-90) East. Take Exit 10 (Auburn) to I-290 East to I-190 North to Exit 5. Take Route 140 North to access road and Wachusett Mountain.

Drive Time: 1.5 hours

With 325,000 skier visits every year, Wachussett is one of New England's most popular ski resorts.

LODGING
Wachusett Village Inn
Westminster, Massachusetts

With colonial furnishings and decorative appointments that reflect the Inn's location near New England's center of furniture design, here you get a true country-inn atmosphere with a wide variety of accommodation options. Seventy-four guest rooms and suites are spread between the main building and cottages. Sixteen rooms feature working fireplaces. Info: 800-342-1905; www.wachusettvillageinn.com

DINING
The Black Diamond Restaurant
On-mountain

With pub-style dining, comfortable booth seating, and great views of the slopes, the Black Diamond offers typical tavern fare: nachos, wraps, burgers and so on. Located on the second floor of the base lodge, it's a great spot for watching the night-skiing action. Info: 978-464-3402

Coppertop Lounge
On-mountain

Comfortable and upscale, the Coppertop is great for warming up by the fire. You can sample from a large selection of renowned local brews, relax over your favorite cocktail, take in a sports event on the large screen TV, or listen to the live music that's performed three nights a week. Info: 978-464-3403

EVENTS
New Year's Eve

With night skiing until midnight, no one does December 31 like Wachusett. Special events all day and night, plus a "morning after" GS race for those able to make it. One of the best on-snow New Year's events in skiing.

Wachusett Mountain Adaptive Skiing Festival

Highlights include instructor clinics, race and technique clinics, and a reception for all participants. Held in mid February. Info: 978-464-2300

Ralph Crowley Classic

A Wachusett tradition and one of New England's most challenging open field ski-racing competitions. The event is held on the classic Smith Walton Trail and is named after the father of Wachusett. Held in early March.

INSIDER TIPS

1) Lifts without lines: The Minuteman Express. Experts think there's nothing here for them, but this less-trafficked lift serves the challenging NASTAR course and Hitchcock, a traditional New England trail.

2) Lifts to take to follow the sun: The resort faces east, so everything gets good sun in the morning, with shadows forming later in the day.

3) What to read to find coupons and deals: The resort's website, www.wachusett.com.

4) Snow stashes: Balance Rock Trail off the summit is the best place to find hidden fluff.

5) Parking secret: Reserved parking is available online (wachusett.com) for $10. It's your best bet, as the lots tend to crowd up.

6) Finest meal for the lowest fare: For the money, the Black Diamond's NASTAR Nachos can't be beat.

SKIING NEAR BOSTON

Blue Hills Ski Area

CANTON, MASSACHUSETTS

From the chairlift at Blue Hills, it feels as if you can reach out and touch the gleaming skyline of Boston. With a little over 300 vertical feet and a handful of runs too short to get you to the chorus of that song running through your head, Blue Hills is little more than a neighborhood hill, conveniently located just off the Route 128 beltway. But during primetime hours, this tiny ski area—built by the Civilian Conservation Corps in the 1930s—hums like an MTA train at rush hour. (In fact, you can reach it by city bus.)

Not too long ago, Blue Hills was a place in desperate need of some work. Enter Al and Walter Endriunas, a couple of construction-company owners who also own Ragged Mountain Ski Area in New Hampshire. Instead of laying out cash for the right to operate it, the Endriunases, who skied here as kids, signed an agreement with the Metropolitan District Commission, which owns Blue Hills, to make much-needed capital improvements. Already, snowmaking upgrades have made a big difference.

VITAL STATS

SUMMIT: 635 feet
VERTICAL DROP: 310 feet
SKIABLE ACRES: 60
BEGINNER: 30%
INTERMEDIATE: 40%
ADVANCED: 30%
SNOWMAKING: 90% coverage
AVG. ANNUAL SNOWFALL: 50 in.
LIFTS: 5; 1 double, 4 surface lifts
TERRAIN PARKS/HALFPIPES:
 1 terrain park, no halfpipes
INFO: 781-828-5070;
 www.thenewbluehills.com

Al Endriunas is up-front about his ulterior motive—turning Blue Hills into a conveyor belt that will transport skiers northward to Ragged. Let them learn their turns in Boston, then ski New Hampshire on weekends. Naturally, kids programs are big: Some 1,200 children enroll for skiing and snowboarding lessons in a season. On a typical day, college racers hit the slopes well before 9 A.M. Then the youth programs kick in. At the end of the day, the lights wink on and high-school racers take over, sharing the lift with locals who prefer the fresh air on the slopes to an evening in the gym. Especially when it's this cheap: Lift tickets cost half as much as what you'd pay up north. That makes skiing affordable at "big" Blue—a little hill with a new lease on life. —M.B.

 **GETTING THERE**
From Boston

Take I-93 South to Exit 2B. Merge onto Washington Street (Route 138). Blue Hills is approximately 1 mile on the right.

Drive Time: 1 hour

From Providence

Take I-95 North to Route 128 South. Take Exit 2B. Merge onto Washington Street (Route 138). Blue Hills is approximately 1 mile on the right.

Drive Time: 2.5 hours

Nashoba Valley
WESTFORD, MASSACHUSETTS

Compared to, say, Vail—or practically any other ski area, for that matter—Nashoba Valley is emphatically puny, the merest of anthills: Vertical tops out at an unwhopping 240 feet.

But it's a big deal to the thousands of kids who learn, train, or just plain enjoy themselves here in a pastoral suburb only 25 miles from Boston. Their parents like it, too, as scores of adults participate faithfully in the weeknight racing series. Nashoba even has its own resident fanatic, Chet Paradise, who, with his altimeter watch, logged 1.2 million vertical feet a couple of seasons ago—an average of 70 runs every day Nashoba was open that year.

"He's the only real hardcore," says Al Fletcher. Fletcher manages the area with his father, Al Sr., the pop behind this mom-and-pop operation since it opened in 1964—and dad to Olympian racer Pam Fletcher, who grew up tearing down Nashoba's gentle slopes.

VITAL STATS

SUMMIT: 440 feet
VERTICAL DROP: 240 feet
SKIABLE ACRES: 60
BEGINNER: 25%
INTERMEDIATE: 50%
ADVANCED: 25%
SNOWMAKING: 100% coverage
AVG. ANNUAL SNOWFALL: 50 in.
LIFTS: 9; 3 triples, 1 double, 4 surface lifts, 1 magic carpet
TERRAIN PARKS/HALFPIPES: no terrain parks, no halfpipes
INFO: 978-692-3033; www.skinashoba.com

"Most people come for the convenience," says Al Jr. "They like the fact that it's as easy as going out to dinner. Plus, they find it less intimidating than the big areas." Having put off my visit until the tail end of the season (mid

MASSACHUSETTS

March), I wasn't so sure about that last part. Unintimidating? The view down Bull Run, where the local prep schools compete, looked downright scary—and I'd just come back from Vail. Maneuvering a beige mosaic of spongy slush, I decided my snowplow could use some work—in the interest of research, of course. Then I followed an aural trail of shrieks and laughter over to the more northerly slopes, where a couple of guys shirking work finessed some smooth moves and hordes of kids careened to screams of "Wait up! Wait up!" I decided to play ministering angel to one lad who was unsuccessfully attempting to mono-ski rather than climb uphill to retrieve his errant gear. "I'm having a hard time turning, too," I confided, handing over the detritus of his yard sale. He looked horrified. "I can turn," he answered haughtily. "They ought to put out more snow." It was my turn to be appalled. Was I staring into the implacable consumerist face of skiing's future? Just then, another boy whizzed past us. "Dad-Dad-Dad-Dad!" he called; it came out like one name. "There was this puddle?" he huffed, catching up. "And I water skied!"

Come rain, sleet, or mud, there will always be joy in Nashoba Valley. —S.M.

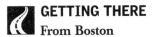 ## GETTING THERE
From Boston

Take Route 2 West to Concord Circle. Take Route 2A/119 to Powers Road and Nashoba Valley.

Drive Time: 1 hour

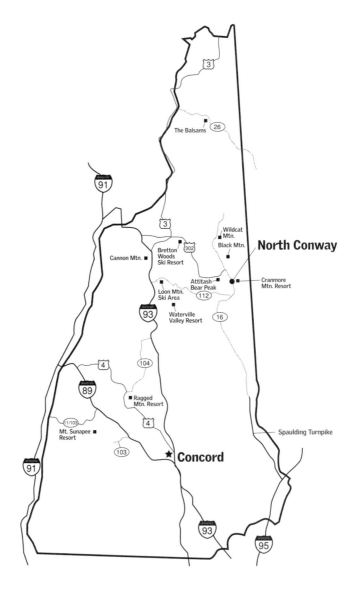

The Balsams 26

91

3

Wildcat
Mtn.
Black Mtn.

North Conway

302

Bretton
Woods
Ski Resort

Cannon Mtn.

Attitash
Bear Peak

Cranmore
Mtn. Resort

Loon Mtn.
Ski Area

112

93

Waterville
Valley Resort

16

104

4

89

Ragged
Mtn. Resort

11/103

4

Mt. Sunapee
Resort

Spaulding Turnpike

103

★ **Concord**

91

93

95

New Hampshire

SKI MAGAZINE'S GUIDE TO NEW ENGLAND AND QUEBEC

NEW HAMPSHIRE

Attitash Bear Peak

BARTLETT, NEW HAMPSHIRE

Attitash Bear Peak is Mount Washington Valley's largest four-season resort. Boston-area families flock to this friendly spot just outside of North Conway, New Hampshire, drawn by its children's programs, snow quality, and service-oriented employees. "A ski area I always know will be good," says one *SKI* Magazine reader. Located partially in the White Mountain National Forest and with views of Mt. Washington and the Presidential Range, Attitash Bear Peak offers a true sampling of New England skiing, from the classic narrow trails on Attitash to the wide-body cruisers of Bear Peak. The peaks are distinct, with separate base areas, yet are connected by trails. Though neither Attitash, with a 1,750-foot vertical drop, nor Bear Peak, with a 1,450-foot vertical, ranks as a big mountain, together they add up to a lot of variety and a lot of skiing. The downside of Attitash is getting uphill. "Take out the triple and put in a quad," advises a *SKI* reader. That's wishful thinking, as the resort is owned by the cash-strapped American Skiing Company, which in better days developed adjacent Bear Peak. With two high-speed quads and wide fall-line trails, Bear Peak is the yin to Attitash's yang. Bear Peak's calling card is four top-to-bottom cruisers that ski longer than they appear. Here, too, are 30 acres of gladed terrain and the slopeside Grand Summit Hotel. Attitash Bear Peak's location in the Mount Washington Valley means plenty of lodging and dining options, as well as more than 120 tax-free outlet and specialty stores.

VITAL STATS

SUMMIT: 2,350 feet

VERTICAL DROP: 1,750 feet

SKIABLE ACRES: 280

BEGINNER: 20%

INTERMEDIATE: 47%

ADVANCED/EXPERT: 33%

SNOWMAKING: 97% coverage

AVG. ANNUAL SNOWFALL: 142 in.

LIFTS: 12; 3 quads, 3 triples, 3 doubles, 3 surface lifts

TERRAIN PARKS/HALFPIPES: 1 terrain park, 1 halfpipe

INFO: 603-374-2368; www.attitash.com

SKIING IT

Lifts officially open at 8 A.M., but regulars know to be in line by 7:45. I grabbed an early breakfast at the hotel, headed outside, grabbed my skis from the ski check and glided into line at the Flying Bear high-speed quad. By 7:50, I was zipping toward the summit. With an early start, you can get in a lot of skiing before the lines form around 10 A.M.

Intermediates and experts will find some of the best cruising trails in New England at Bear Peak. The trails ski longer than those at Attitash and are wide enough to forgive less-experienced skiers. Most of the cruisers drop in stages: Just when you think you might be in over your head, the terrain mellows and lets you catch your breath before the next pitch.

I warmed up on Wandering Skis, a meandering nearly two-mile intermediate trail that could pass for advanced-beginner were it not for a tricky S-turn pitch at the top. Next up was Illusion, an appropriately named trail that seemed to go on and on, and without the traffic of its steeper siblings, Avenger, Mythmaker and Kachina.

I skied over to the Attitash base area, collected my friend Gayle, and headed to Flying Yankee, a new high-speed quad that only reaches mid mountain but accesses some of Attitash's best terrain. We cycled on the fall-line trails with consistent pitches—Moat, Ptarmigan, Spillway, White Horse and the always-bumpy Grand Stand—till our legs cried for mercy. Then we took an early lunch at Ptarmigan's, a pub-style restaurant on the third floor of the Attitash base lodge.

After lunch, we headed to the summit on the Top Notch double, a.k.a. the Hall chair. (It helps to know that locals refer to the lifts by the names of their manufacturers: The Borvigs are the side-by-side doubles, the Hall is the Top Notch double, and the C-Tec is the Summit triple.) The triple reaches the true summit, but if you take the double you'll only miss one trail (albeit a good one: Wilfred's Gawm) and a rather flat access area.

We began with Tightrope, a narrow, double-black cruiser that, like me, was showing signs of afternoon wear. Next we headed down Saco, dropping off the edge on Tim's Trauma, which, given the now heavily falling snow, was a mixed bag: scraped off here, clumps of snow there, sweet powder in between. Tim's drops into Lower Cathedral, an unavoidable run-out that one regular compares to Boston's Central Artery at rush hour: lots of hotshots zipping around breakdowns and Sunday drivers.

The early start and nonstop skiing eventually took their toll (besides, I heard outlet stores calling me), so I left Gayle and began making my way back to Bear Peak. While it's a straight shot from Bear Peak to Attitash, the reverse isn't. If I'd known it would require three lift rides and 45 minutes, I would have taken the shuttle.

The next morning, I rose early and peeked out the window—yes!—at least a foot of powder on the deck. By 7:40, I was in the quad line with a couple dozen other powder hounds, including mountain-ops director Russ Van Deursen. "I can get you first tracks till noon," he promised. I grinned, and we were off.

I followed Russ as he sliced through a wind-blown cornice on Kachina and maneuvered through the bumps, the wind whipping the displaced powder into a flurry. The drifts were so deep they stopped me dead, twice. We dropped into Lumberyard and later Broken Arrow, both sheltered glades where the snow sprinkled through the branches, caressing our faces.

After cruising Illusion and Mythmaker, we headed to Attitash for a run on Wilfred's Gawm. Though it was now midmorning, we still found untracked lines. We enjoyed more first tracks on the edges of Saco and Idiot's Option. Hunky Dory, an intermediate trail off Upper Cathedral, rewarded us with more unblemished powder, and we hit White Horse just as it was opened. By late morning, my legs were shot. −H.N.

FAMILY MATTERS

If you want lessons or have kids in tow, head for the Attitash base and unload at the Adventure Center, a godsend for first-timers and parents. This large, modern building houses ticket sales, rentals, childcare and a snack bar. The new Perfect Turn Discovery Center, a state-of-the-art ski and snowboard school, is also located here. Isolated from the intimidating buzz of the main base area, newbies are coddled every step of the way through the daunting process of going skiing for the first time: getting dressed and equipped, riding the lift and, of course, skiing down the hill. A shuttle bus serving both bases and the hotel stops at the front door. The beginner-only slopes and lifts are out the back door.

Once they've graduated from daycare (and Attitash has done daycare well for decades now), children can start out skiing in the Buddy Bear Kids Program. Designed for four to six year olds, this program incorporates the American Skiing Company's Perfect Turn teaching methods. Specially trained pros lead each group first through the fun and non-threatening Story Land–themed terrain garden, and then move them up onto the gentle terrain via a Magic Carpet lift.

For children not quite ready for that but ready to taste the on-snow life, Attitash offers the Tiny Turns Program. In it, three to five year olds are introduced to the snow in a private, one-on-one clinic. Older kids (seven to 12) can enroll in the Adventure Kids Program for explorations of the mountains or advanced mogul skiing and halfpipe riding.

In terms of family, the best thing about Attitash Bear Peak may be the layout. A traditional New England mountain, it always empties out to the same two base areas—Attitash and Bear Peak. It's easy to let kids who are ready for a little freedom take off. You know you'll be bumping into them constantly.

GETTING THERE
From Boston

Take I-95 North to Exit 4. Take the Spaulding Turnpike/ Route 16 North through Conway Village and into Glen. Take Route 302 West to Attitash Bear Peak.

Drive Time: 2.5 hours

From Portland

Take Route 302 West. In North Conway Route 302 West and Route 16 North intersect and merge. Follow route 16/302 into Glen. Take Route 302 West to Attitash Bear Peak.

Drive Time: 1.5 hours

LODGING
The Grand Summit Resort Hotel
Bartlett, New Hampshire

The Grand Summit Resort Hotel at Attitash Bear Peak is fairly representative of the general Grand Summit blueprint: huge atrium lobby with a massive stone hearth, spiffy rooms ranging from standard studios to luxury suites, conference facilities (New Hampshire's most spacious), a heated outdoor pool-cum-hot tub, health club plus cafe and an on-site restaurant offering good, affordable New American fare. Oh, and of course, slopeside access. Like a landlocked ocean liner, this hotel meets every conceivable need, so you can concentrate, pleasurably, on the slopes. It is perhaps indicative of the staff's will to please that the chef canvassed the dumpsters to prove to management that guests would appreciate in-house pizza delivery: Hence the afterthought addition of a wood-fired oven. Info: 603-374-1900 —S.M.

The Bernerhof
Glen, New Hampshire

Our first duty upon arrival at this turreted Victorian beauty was to snap a memento photo for a pair of departing honeymooners. It's that kind of place. The second was to leap into the double whirlpool in our private turret to soak our slope-stressed muscles. And third, to partake of the kind of hearty Middle European fare—escargot, wiener schnitzel, Toblerone fondue—you can only get away with on a ski trip.

Long prized for its restaurant (which now operates independently as Prince Place) and its perennially cheerful Black Bear Pub, The Bernerhof has gone contemporary-luxurious while retaining its old-fashioned charm. The hot tubs are a tip off: six of the nine rooms have one. One of the rooms that doesn't is a multi-bedded family suite—a thoughtful nod to the budget-minded. Rather than shoehorn in modern amenities, long-time owners Sharon and Ted Wroblewski raised the roof, rendering the third-floor quarters especially appealing, with many pleasant corners. The decor tends toward catchall Victoriana—not too cluttered and decidedly comfortable. Stay four nights and your final breakfast will be brought to you in bed, complete with flowers and champagne. Info: 603-383-9132; 800-548-8007; www.bernerhofinn.com –S.M.

 DINING

Glen Junction Restaurant
Glen, New Hampshire

Laid-back but warm and friendly, Glen Junction serves breakfast all day and hearty, basic lunches in the afternoon. The train motif features old train sets, some running, throughout the restaurant. Kids love it. Info: 603-383-9660

Red Parka Pub
Glen, New Hampshire

To old-time Attitash skiers, it's almost a sin to visit the area and not stop in at the Parka. The restaurant side is a classic steakhouse with a twist. The prime rib has been raved about for almost three decades, and the newer pasta-based dishes with unique spices are winners, too. The giant salad bar and nightly specials round things out. On the pub side, look for a big crowd after skiing each day. The walls are crammed with Mount Washington Valley memorabilia, and the bands are always good. Info: 603-383-4344

NEW HAMPSHIRE

EVENTS
The Polar Express

The famed children's book *The Polar Express*, written by Chris Van Allsburg, comes to life weekends in December. Families can hop aboard The Polar Express (the Conway Scenic Railroad the rest of the year) from the center of North Conway. The experience includes an evening train ride and quality time with elves, and, of course, Santa himself. Info: 603-447-3100; www.polarexpress.org

The Lenny Clarke Celebrity Ski Classic to benefit the Genesis Fund

Attitash Bear Peak, comedian Lenny Clarke, movie and TV celebrities, and New England sports heroes join forces to raise money for the Genesis Fund, which assists New England area children born with birth defects, mental retardation, and genetic diseases. Activities include a banquet, auction and a recreational team ski race. Held early February.

Annual Red Parka Pub Challenge Cup

For over 30 years, this has been the race to win in the Mount Washington Valley for big prizes, publicity and, of course, bragging rights. It's the premier local event, but fun for visitors to cheer on as well. Held mid March.

Spring Mania
Attitash Bear Peak On-Snow Golf Tournament

Costume-clad teams of four drive, pitch and putt their way through a nine-hole course designed by the resort's master groomers—complete with elevated tee boxes, bunkers and greens. Live music for everyone throughout the day on the Attitash Base Lodge Snow Stage. Held late March.

INSIDER TIPS

1) Lifts without lines: Flying Bear quad at Bear Peak is never crowded. Abenaki quad at Bear is away from the base lodges and therefore less trafficked as well.

2) Lifts to take to follow the sun: Take the Summit Triple chair and ski Saco/Ammonoosuc on Attitash for morning sun or ski Morning Star (not named by accident), Snow Dancer and Kachina Falls off the Flying Bear

NEW HAMPSHIRE

or Abenaki quads. In the afternoon, take the Summit triple to Northwest Passage for the best sun, or hit Avenger and Illusion off the Flying Bear.

3) What to read to find coupons and deals: *The Mountain Ear* and *The Conway Daily Sun.*

4) Snow stashes: Idiot's Option at Attitash. Trillium, Upper Myth Maker and all of the glades on Bear.

5) Parking secret: Premium parking at Attitash will cost you $10. The parking at Bear is free with perfectly convenient access and little or no hassle.

Bretton Woods Ski Resort

BRETTON WOODS, NEW HAMPSHIRE

For years, Bretton Woods was known as a small resort that catered to low-level skiers with gentle terrain and a stress-free atmosphere. In 1998, the resort embarked on a five-year expansion plan, and skiers who previously dismissed the area are now rediscovering it. While the resort has expanded its terrain (it's now the largest in New Hampshire with 375 skiable acres), enlarged its lodge and added high-speed lifts, it continues to attract a laid-back crowd that appreciates its remote but magnificent setting and family-friendly programs. Thanks to the addition of a second high-speed quad, the previously minimal liftlines are now virtually nonexistent. And that feeling of elbowroom extends to the trails. Bretton Woods "never feels crowded," says one *SKI* Magazine reader. "The design of the trails makes you feel like you are the only person skiing." Though still renowned as an "intermediate paradise," the resort is scoring points with advanced skiers (if not experts) for its new West Mountain glades. More glades were cut on the

VITAL STATS

SUMMIT: 3,100 feet

VERTICAL DROP: 1,500 feet

SKIABLE ACRES: 375

BEGINNER: 29%

INTERMEDIATE: 39%

ADVANCED/EXPERT: 32%

SNOWMAKING: 95% coverage

AVG. ANNUAL SNOWFALL: 200 in.

LIFTS: 9; 4 high-speed quads, 1 fixed quad, 1 triple, 1 double, 1 surface lift, 1 rope tow

TERRAIN PARKS/HALFPIPES: 1 terrain park, 1 halfpipe

INFO: 603-278-3320; www.brettonwoods.com

steeper terrain between Mt. Stickney and Mt. Rosebrook. This may assuage those *SKI* readers who in the past complained that there was "no real challenge for advanced skiers, and black-diamond trails are in the low to intermediate range." Truthfully, most skiers don't come here for the challenge; they come for the entire resort experience. The Mount Washington Hotel, first opened in 1902 and winterized for the 1999–2000 season, is the grandest and most historic lodge in the East, with Mount Washington and the Presidential Range as its backdrop. No wonder visitors praise the scenery as "outstanding," calling it the "best view in New England."

SKIING IT

Though we hadn't skied here before, we'd heard that the slopes of Bretton Woods are gentle. This proved to be an understatement. Starting out on the east side and working west, we encountered abundant green-circle terrain, only occasionally bordering on blue (though the trail map says otherwise). Molly, a cautious intermediate, was never outside her comfort zone. Meanwhile, I was having hard time getting up enough speed to bend my skis into an arc. This, of course, makes Bretton Woods an intermediate's paradise and a wonderful playground for children, though it might leave experts cold. The West Mountain expansion does offer more challenge, though. And if that's still not enough, the resort has a solution that will appease even the most aggressive daredevil: Through an exchange with neighboring, state-owned Cannon Mountain ski area, hotel guests can avail themselves of what is often described as New Hampshire's most intimidating terrain. Multi-day tickets are interchangeable between the two, and shuttles run twice daily.

The view from the top of the West Mountain terrain, just above where the new quad now terminates, spans 360 degrees and is a perfect 10—you can even see Stowe's trails way off to the west in Vermont. And in a pure Bretton Woods touch, an old cog railway car has been helicoptered in to serve as a warming hut—put to new use after years of climbing Mount Washington.

The West Mountain terrain is a huge addition for Bretton Woods, increasing its skiable acreage to 375. It's now the largest area in New Hampshire, and trail work has already begun on its East Mountain expansion, which will open up roughly another 100 acres. —J.C.

NEW HAMPSHIRE

FAMILY MATTERS

Bretton Woods' first plus for families is its terrain. Seldom can you find a big mountain with a pitch so gentle the entire family can ski nearly every trail together. And while Bretton Woods has its share of wide-open cruisers, it has as many, if not more, trails that, while mellow, are pure New England. Kids can ski along with Mom and Dad and duck in and out of the woods, never veering too far from sight, but feeling adventurous nonetheless.

Then there are the programs. The Babes in the Woods Nursery takes children aged two months to five years. For an introduction to sliding on snow, there's the Snow Play and Readiness Program. In it, children from three to five are based at the nursery but also head out for two one-hour lessons each day. Older kids find their action in the Hobbit Program, where they are matched with skiers or boarders their same age and ability, and sent out with instructors to learn and explore the mountain.

GETTING THERE
From Boston

Take I-93 North to Exit 35. Take Route 3 North to Route 302 East. Follow to Bretton Woods.

Drive Time: 2.5 hours

From New York City

Take I-95 North to I-91 North to I-93 South to Exit 40. Take Route 302 East to Bretton Woods.

Drive Time: 6 hours

LODGING
The Mount Washington Hotel
Bretton Woods, New Hampshire

A grand masterpiece of Spanish Renaissance architecture, the Mount Washington Hotel was a two-year labor of love for 250 master craftsmen. Conceived by industrialist Joseph Stickney, this National Historic Landmark opened in 1902 and immediately became a favorite summer haunt for princes, presidents and poets. In 2000, it reopened and became a top choice for those seeking easy ski-resort access and opulent accommodations. In terms of splendor, the Mount Washington stands alone. Rooms are modernized but still have a turn-of-the-century feel. You can

Bretton Woods offers many trails the entire family can ski together.

book a single or a two-bedroom suite (no kitchens, but you won't want them—the dining room is superb). The indoor pool was built nearly 80 years ago. And as you sit in the grand foyer in the evening, you can almost hear the echoes of the high society that filled those hallways for years. Bring a jacket for dinner, but don't worry, you will be relaxed. Info: 800.258.0330; www.mtwashington.com

The Bretton Arms
Bretton Woods, New Hampshire

For a more casual choice, the Bretton Arms, next door to the Mount Washington, is the place. This inn, located on the Nordic trail network (just across the street from the ski area), combines the service and style of a grand hotel with the warmth of a country inn. A National Historic Landmark, the inn has 34 rooms and suites. The dining room and lounge provide a romantic fireside setting and are often used by locals and visitors who come just for dinner and relaxation. A complimentary resort shuttle and access to the sports center are included with the room. Info: 800.258.0330

The Bretton Woods Motor Inn
Bretton Woods, New Hampshire

Located across the street from the Mount Washington Hotel and on the same side of the road as the ski area, the Motor Inn offers an indoor heated pool, Jacuzzi and sauna. All 50 guest rooms have a private patio or balcony overlooking the Mount Washington Hotel and the peaks of the

NEW HAMPSHIRE

Presidential Range. The new Darby's Diner is a retro-style eatery that serves breakfast, lunch, and dinner daily. Room rates include a complimentary resort shuttle and access to the sports center. Info 603.278.1000

The Townhomes at Bretton Woods
Bretton Woods, New Hampshire

The townhomes are located throughout the resort and are a great choice for families who like a "home away from home" when on vacation. Ranging from one to five bedrooms, the townhomes are ideal for couples or families seeking comfort, convenience and privacy. Amenities include fireplaces, full kitchens and baths, living/dining areas, washers and dryers, ski lockers, and outdoor decks. The complimentary resort shuttle and access to the sports center are included in the rental rates. Info: 800.258.0330

DINING
The Main Dining Room of the Mount Washington Hotel
Bretton Woods, New Hampshire

The grand hotel's opulence spills into its dining room. At night, you'll find an elaborate buffet of European and American cuisine, four-course dinners and dancing to live entertainment. In the mornings, you can start the day like royalty with a feast of eggs benedict, french toast and assorted fresh fruit and pastries. The menu changes daily. Info: 603-278-1000

Stickney's Restaurant

Located on the patio level of The Mount Washington Hotel, Stickney's serves fresh salads, sandwiches, burgers and delicious homemade soups. Info: 800.258.0330

The Bretton Arms
Bretton Woods, New Hampshire

Across the street from the ski area, the Bretton Arms has an intimate dining room with a fireplace. Breakfasts are hearty, and dinners—with offerings like filet mignon, roast duck, veal picatta and fresh seafood—are top-notch. Reservations are required. Info: 603-278-3000

Fabyan's Station Restaurant and Lounge
Bretton Woods, New Hampshire

Across the street from the ski area, this renovated railroad station serves lunch and dinner daily. For lunch you get typical warm-your-bones fare like buffalo wings, nachos, soups, sandwiches, burgers, chili and stuffed spuds. Dinner—fried chicken, chicken primavera, ribs and the like—is comfort food, too. Info: 603-278-2222

Darby's Restaurant and Lounge
Bretton Woods, New Hampshire
Located in the Bretton Woods Motor Inn, Darby's bakes handmade pizzas and builds a variety of sub sandwiches. Info: 603-278-1500

 EVENTS
A North Country Christmas
A weekend of events that includes selecting your own fresh-cut tree at the Rocks Estate and an assortment of musical and children's events. As you ski, you can even drop all your gifts off at a gift-wrap station, and they'll be ready for you at the end of your day. Held the first weekend of December.

Annual New Year's Eve Slopeside Celebration
Night skiing, a dinner buffet, a rock-n-roll party featuring a live band, party favors, champagne for the adults and a torchlight parade. Fireworks bring things to a close.

Geschmossel 15-kilometer Classical Ski Race
This classical-style cross-country ski race (no skating allowed) takes place on the Ammonoosuc Trail Network at Bretton Woods' Nordic ski area. One of the oldest citizens' races in New England, it is held in late January and begins with a mass start at 11 A.M. Info: 603-278-3322

Angel Flight Celebrity Cup Weekend
Held in mid March, a full weekend of social activities, culminating with a fund-raising ski race with celebrity team captains to benefit Angel Flight, an organization that provides air transportation for people in need of medical care. Past celebrities have included *Extra's* Barry Nolan, extreme skiers Wayne Wong and Kristen Ulmer, and *Survivor's* Dr. Sean.

Spring Festival
Held in early April, it's a weekend of spring skiing, floral demonstrations, live music, culinary expos, wine tastings, and much more. The week-

NEW HAMPSHIRE

end also features the annual Bretton Woods Beach Party with spring skiing, island-style entertainment, a barbecue, slush-pool-skimming competition.

INSIDER TIPS

1) Lifts without lines: In 2002, the resort turned the West Mountain quad into a high-speed detachable, making it the place for shorter lines.

2) Lifts to take to follow the sun: Start the day on the Bethlehem Express high-speed quad and take a quick warm-up down to Fabyan's Express triple. From the summit take any trail toward the east to face the morning sun. Spend the afternoon exploring West Mountain and you're likely to find plenty of soft snow.

3) What to read to find discounts and coupons: *The Mountain Ear*, the weekly news and lifestyle journal of Mount Washington Valley.

4) Snow stashes: Without a doubt, Rosebrook Canyon. You can also find a stash or two in some of the West Mountain Glades, like Cliff's Cliff or Wild West.

5) Parking secret: The secret is to not use your car. Pick up your lift ticket at the front desk of your hotel and take the free shuttle directly to the lift.

6) Finest meal for the lowest fare: The Slopeside Restaurant, located on the second level of the Bretton Woods base lodge.

Cannon Mountain
FRANCONIA, NEW HAMPSHIRE

Cannon is a living reminder of how skiing used to be. And for its many devotees, it's an example of how skiing should be still: no glitz and no glamour—just plenty of good skiing and good company. Stop in the weathered warming hut at the top of Cannon's 70-person aerial tram, and you'll likely hear small talk about the good old days, when the Hochgebirge Ski Club was formed in 1933 or when Jean-Claude Killy and Nancy Greene raced here in the late 1960s. Step outside the hut and head down Upper Cannon, a classic, winding New England trail, and the good old days won't seem so long ago. Other than recent on-mountain upgrades–seven new trials with snowmaking–and the new Notch View Lodge, not much has changed at the resort in the past 60 years. And for relaxed accommodations, skiers should head to nearby Franconia or Sugar Hill. Local lore has it that esteemed poet Robert Frost composed his verse "The Road Not Taken" while living in Franconia.

SKIING IT

The Cannon parking lot is already half full when we arrive, 15 minutes after leaving the inn. I am struck by how large the mountain is and how small the base development seems. A lodge, a couple of smaller adjacent buildings, a new daycare center, and that's it. Out of sight down the road are a couple of additional buildings–the tramway base station and the New England Ski Museum–but the overall impression of the place is that you come to ski, and just ski. So we do.

We warm up on some lower-slope beginner runs like Toss-Up and Lower Cannon, finding the March snow coarse but well-groomed. Then we jump on the new Peabody Express quad chair. A vast improvement over the old "Slowbody" double it replaced, it zips us three-quarters of the way up the mountain and into the intermediate playground there. Runs like Middle Cannon, Big Link, Middle Ravine and a nice little cut-through called Spookie are for the most part a lot of fun. The snow is piled into bumps here and there, and a few icy patches gleam in the morning light, but there is plenty of good stuff at the edges of the trails to make it enjoyable.

After a lunch break of bagels and Cokes, we head back up the Peabody Express, then cut over on a short stretch of Big Link to connect with the Cannonball Express quad. The Cannonball offers a bird's-eye view of the Profile trail–a steep, bumpy black-diamond that I put on my list for later that day–before depositing us near the summit, slightly above the tram station. We stand for a few minutes looking out across the notch at hulk-

VITAL STATS

SUMMIT: 4,186 feet

VERTICAL DROP: 2,146 feet

SKIABLE ACRES: 165

BEGINNER: 17%

INTERMEDIATE: 48%

ADVANCED/EXPERT: 35%

SNOWMAKING: 97% coverage

AVG. ANNUAL SNOWFALL: 150 in.

LIFTS: 9; one 70-person Aerial Tramway, 2 detachable quads, 1 quad, 3 triples, 1 rope tow, 1 magic carpet

TERRAIN PARKS/HALFPIPES: 1 terrain park, 1 halfpipe

INFO: 603-823-8800; www.cannonmt.com

NEW HAMPSHIRE

ing Mount Lafayette, then we head for the narrow, twisty, ungroomed trails Cannon likes to tout as its remaining old-school runs—Taft Slalom, and Upper, Middle and Lower Hardscrabble.

Taft Slalom is a narrow but manageable intermediate trail that heads straight for the trails of old Mittersill (a now-defunct ski area that is accessible from Cannon) before veering into the black-diamond Upper Hardscrabble. Upper, with its icy patches and generally gnarly aspect, humbles me; I hack my way down, followed by the equally snaggly Middle, in a series of linked face plants and sitzmarks. Despite my tortured descent, I can see the appeal; on a powder day (they happen here more often than you think), these narrow, twisty trails would offer serious fun—a little bit of Vermont's Mad River Glen transplanted to New Hampshire.

Eventually I head to the top of Profile, look down, think better of it, then cut over to Vista Way, a mountaintop intermediate cruiser that hooks up with Middle Cannon. On the lower mountain, I skid down the fringes of the black-diamond Zoomer as slalom racers in the middle of the run make it look easy. As we are contemplating our next move at the bottom, it starts to mist—a perfect excuse to hop on the tram, a mile-long marvel that opened in 1980 on the same site of North America's first tramway, which opened back in 1938. The ride gives us a slightly different view of Mount Lafayette, which is slowly being obscured by the low gray clouds settling over the valley. It also gives us a moment to reflect—and Cannon has a way of making you do that. Part of the reason is the New England Ski Museum, a tiny and pleasantly cluttered place that sits next to the tramway's base. New Hampshire was arguably the cradle of skiing in America in the 1920s and '30s, and the museum does a great job of capturing the early, innocent days of the sport. That's something you can still feel at Cannon, and it's part of what makes Cannon so special. Even when it's misty outside. —s.s.

FAMILY MATTERS

Cannon is no Disney World, but that does not mean families can't feel comfortable here. First off, the layout is perfect. Send the kids off skiing and you know, every run, they'll either end up at the base lodge or the bottom of the tram. The Brookside Learning Center, newly minted in 1999, is set apart from the big runs, which gives kids and first-timers a quiet, non-threatening place to start out. The ski school and daycare building are both an easy shot from the Peabody lift, so parents can easily check in on kids and jump back on a lift to ski.

Ski school works like this: Three-and four-year-olds head out for short lessons and then come back indoors to play in the Cannon Tykes program. Six-to nine-year-olds get a longer day of skiing but plenty of hot-chocolate breaks in the Cannon Kids program. And nine-to twelve-year-olds tear up the mountain in the Mountain Explorers program. For kids who really take to skiing fast, the Franconia Ski Club, one of the area's most respected racing programs, calls Cannon home.

After skiing, families once had little to do at Cannon. Now there's a tubing-specific lift that allows kids and adults to tube their hearts out.

GETTING THERE
From Boston

Take I-93 North to Exit 34C. Follow signs to Cannon Mountain. Drive Time: 2.5 hours

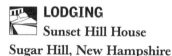

LODGING
Sunset Hill House
Sugar Hill, New Hampshire

Arguably the most posh yet most comfortable lodging near Cannon, the Sunset Hill House has direct views of the ski area and five different mountain ranges. Cross-country skiing and snowshoeing trails and equipment for both are offered on site. The lodge also has Jacuzzis, fireplaces, suites and discount lift tickets. Info: 800-786-4455; www.sunsethillhouse.com

Parker's Motel
Lincoln, New Hampshire

This is the first motel south of Cannon Mountain and it's quite likely the most affordable. Amenities are basic, but there is an indoor Jacuzzi and sauna, and the place is always squeaky clean. Ski-and-stay packages are available, as are two- and three-bedroom units. Info: 800-766-6835; www.parkersmotel.com

DINING
Woodwards
Lincoln, New Hampshire

With a choice of 35 entrées on their menu, Woodwards has something

to please everyone. Choose from prime rib, hand-cut steaks and fresh seafood or lobster. Each dinner includes homemade desserts made on the property by the staff's full-time baker. Info: 603-745-8141, 800-635-8968

Franconia Village House Restaurant
Franconia, New Hampshire

Known as the locals' spot for après-ski, the Village House is the kind of place where you feel perfectly at home in your ski pants, and the food is as comforting as the atmosphere. Signature dishes are the certified Angus Beef and everything on the late-night menu, but don't miss the munchies like nachos and wings. Info: 603-823-5405

EVENTS
Insider Demo Day

To participate in this equipment demo, attendees must pre-purchase tickets via Cannon's website. Once that's done, skiers are treated to a day on the mountain and a bevy of demo gear. Usually held early November.

Jack and Sam Race

Named after the resort's ski-school director and Sam Adams Beer, this dual-slalom race is held in February for skiers 21 and older. Prizes and parties follow.

Root Beer Rally Race

A race open to all ages but only more advanced skiers, this event is held every March and is sponsored by the Woodstock Brewery, which brews root beer for the event.

Crash Test Dummy Race

Each year in late March, Cannonites build the "perfect beast" for skiing—a dummy that they launch down the mountain as a crowd cheers them on. Some are clever—like the one made entirely of brass piping; others are symbolic—like those that look eerily like some political figures.

INSIDER TIPS

1) Lifts without lines: The tram in the morning. While it was once over-crowded, the new high-speed quad at the base has pulled people away

Ride to the top of 4,186-foot Cannon Mountain in the 70-passenger Aerial Tram for views of Maine, Vermont and Canada.

from the tram. That said, the longest timed lift line at Cannon in 2002 was 10 minutes, so you're pretty safe no matter what.

2) Lifts to take to follow the sun: Start at the top of the mountain, using the quads. Head to Cannon's "Front Five" midday, and finish on the gentle but still sunny lower terrain.

3) Snow stashes: Mittersill. You have to hike there but baby, it's worth it. Skiing through this abandoned ski area is both eerie and beautiful. And the snow, which seems to pile deeper there, remains untouched for days.

4) Parking secret: Arrive early and park near the tram weekends and holidays to be the first on the mountain with the First Tracks Program. The tram gets you on the mountain at 8:15 A.M., a full 15 minutes before the lifts open.

5) Finest meal for the lowest fare: Woodstock Station. This brewery not only makes great beer, but also serves good food. Try the Croute Root, a ham, turkey and Swiss puff pastry topped with *boursin* cheese.

NEW HAMPSHIRE

Loon Mountain Ski Area

LINCOLN, NEW HAMPSHIRE

Loon Mountain embodies the three L's of good real estate: location, location, location. The two-hour straightshot from Boston wins Loon *SKI* Magazine's top marks for accessibility year after year. But don't think Loon rests on its convenient-commute status. Nestled in New Hampshire's White Mountain National Forest, Loon has worked hard to carve out a niche for always ego-boosting and sometimes challenging skiing and snowboarding. "Loon's grooming is great!" cheers one *SKI* reader. "Great cruising trails!" Long known as the home of powerful snowmaking, impeccable grooming and wide-open acres of cushy trails, Loon tried to expand into more advanced territory. Stalled by anti-expansion locals, the resort turned instead to improving what it already had. Recently additions like an upgraded terrain park have drawn raves, as has a new 15-acre expert glade. Still, most advanced skiers find Loon lacking. "Too tame. I never got a chance to get excited," one *SKI* reader complains. The resort recently unveiled seven acres of gentle, rolling tree skiing to lure beginner skiers into the woods. While the nearby town of Lincoln lacks spunk, Loon offers on-mountain events aplenty. There's tubing day and night, those crazy snow bikes, and an après-ski Slopeside Adventure Center with bonfires, skating, a climbing wall and daily family entertainment. And then there are the crowds, *SKI* readers' number-one complaint. While Loon remains relatively quiet on weekdays, the easy drive from Boston packs it on weekends. Advice? Hit the gondola early and stay on the upper mountain the rest of the day. Loon is never going to be a place where jarring steeps take your breath away, but it has become a resort where the gentle mix of easy access, forgiving pitches and fabulous grooming can be positively breathtaking.

VITAL STATS

SUMMIT: 3,050 feet

VERTICAL DROP: 2,100 feet

SKIABLE ACRES: 275

BEGINNER: 20%

INTERMEDIATE: 64%

ADVANCED/EXPERT: 16%

SNOWMAKING: 99% coverage

AVG. ANNUAL SNOWFALL: 130 in.

LIFTS: 10; 1 gondola, 1 quad, 2 triples, 3 doubles, 3 surface lifts

TERRAIN PARKS/HALFPIPES: 3 terrain parks, 2 halfpipes

INFO: 603-745-8111; www.loonmtn.com

Located in New Hampshire's White Mountain National Forest, Loon Mountain is just a two-hour drive from Boston.

SKIING IT

Loon is an intermediate's mountain, with 64 percent of the runs designated blue. The bulk of the beginner's terrain is to the far right (looking up the mountain) off the Kissin' Cousin double chair, but novices can also work their way down from the summit on Upper Bear Claw to Lower Bear Claw—a trip worth taking for the views alone.

The steepest trails, such as bumped-up Flume and rolling Upper Walking Boss, are off North Peak, accessible from the gondola and the North Peak triple chair. The gondola opens at 8 A.M. If you arrive at 7:30, you'll find hardcores already in line to catch the first car up. But forget about the gondola after 10 A.M.; it's jammed. Instead, take the Seven Brothers triple chair and then the East Basin double or the North Peak triple to get to the summit. Ski the top half of the mountain until lunchtime.

In the afternoon, ski the intermediate cruisers off the Kancamangus quad. Runs such as the groomed Lower Picked Rock and the meandering, "skiers only" Blue Ox catch great late-afternoon sun. Some of the best skiing is on Sunday afternoon, after all the type A's have pointed their Saabs south and you have the mountain almost to yourself. If it has snowed overnight, you may even find midday freshies on Basin Street, an intermediate run off the summit that doesn't get nearly as much traffic as black-diamond Angel Street. If there is enough snow to open it, Triple Trouble—an ungroomed, old-time twisty trail—is the best expert run on the mountain. You can reach it from the East Basin chair or the gondola. The East Basin lift, by the way, often has no lift lines even when the North Peak chair is jammed.

Twenty miles of cross-country trails flank the resort as well. The East Ridge trails are the most interesting. The resort's Nordic Center offers rentals, instruction and guided tours. Snowshoeing gear and skates are also available there for rent. —M.L.N.

FAMILY MATTERS

Loon does pay close attention to families, and it starts with the "Threedom Pass," one of the best lift-ticket deals around. For one flat rate you get access not just to Loon, but also to nearby Waterville Valley and Cranmore mountains. While rates differ for age groups and weekday versus all-week passes, the most you'll pay for an entire season at all three mountains combined is $500. Now that's family friendly.

Loon backs the deal up with good programs for kids. The Loon daycare takes children from six weeks to eight years old. The daycare facility has large indoor playrooms, an outdoor play area and a quiet area for naps. Lunch is included for one-year-olds and up.

P.K. Boo Bear Camp is a new program for three-year-olds only. The program includes daycare and up to two hours of lessons for children who have never skied before. Children who can already ski will be placed with the four-year-olds at the discretion of the staff.

The Ski Mite Group Lesson is for four-to five-year-olds, and features specially trained coaches who guide kids through age-appropriate on-snow activities. The full-hour lesson is perfect for kids not ready for the all-day program.

Kinderbear Camp comes into play for four-, five-, and six-year-olds who are ready to hit the mountain for a full day. It includes morning and afternoon lessons, lunch, breaks for hot-chocolate and snacks and an all-mountain lift pass.

Adventure Camp is for kids seven through twelve and up and includes a full day of lessons, lunch, hot-chocolate and snack breaks and an all-mountain lift ticket. The camp runs from 9:00 A.M. to 2:45 in the afternoon, with early registration opening at 8:30 for parents who want to make first tracks.

GETTING THERE
From Boston

Take I-93 North to Exit 32. Turn left onto Route 112 and follow to Loon Mountain.

Drive Time: 2 hours

NEW HAMPSHIRE

LODGING
Mountain Club on Loon
Loon Mountain, New Hampshire

The only hotel-like, slopeside lodging at Loon, the Mountain Club offers ski-in–ski-out convenience, a restaurant, bar, fitness center, pool and special activities. Rooms, suites and condos are open and airy, with cable TV/VCR, washers and dryers.

 DINING
Earl of Sandwich
Lincoln, New Hampshire

For almost two decades, après ski munchies have been satisfied at Earl of Sandwich, the self-proclaimed "not-so-fast, fast food restaurant" where you can get delicious pizzas, subs, burgers and salads at great prices. The Chicken Pizza is great and vegetarians will dig the Meatless Chili. Info: 603-745-2554

 EVENTS
Independence Day Weekend

Loon uses this big ski weekend to celebrate those who give us independence from Mother Nature–the snowmakers. Events always include a torchlight parade, snowcat rides and fireworks. Held Martin Luther King, Jr. weekend in January.

CASA Winter Golf-on-Snow Open

A fundraiser for the Court Appointed Special Advocates of New Hampshire, this event takes golf to a whole new level, morphing it with skiing for some competitive but hilarious results. Held in February.

Briefcase Race

A fundraiser for the Faulkner Breast Centre in Boston, this event pits teams against one another in a work-attire themed race. Watch nurses, businessmen and even firefighters careen down the course in full gear. Held in March.

Cardboard Box Classic

Teams get together to make racing contraptions out of cardboard. Cash prizes are awarded. Held in March.

NEW HAMPSHIRE

Loon Mountain offers riders wide-open groomed trails and a 1,400 foot superpipe.

Slush Pool Party

Participants do their best to ski or waterski across the pond built in front of the Octagon Lodge. Every year the pond gets bigger. Held in April.

INSIDER TIPS

1) Lifts without lines: North Peak triple for advanced to intermediate skiers. Seven Brothers triple for intermediates and below.

2) Lifts to take to follow the sun: Start at the North Peak, move to the terrain off the gondola, then move to the West side.

3) What to read to find coupons and discounts: *Ski Week*.

4) Snow stashes: Any of the tree-skiing areas, or on the sides of Coolidge Street.

5) Secret parking: At Loon, you can buy a parking season pass — this will get you premiere parking on the other side of the children's center. Or you can get there early and park on the west side of the main parking lot, next to the quad.

6) Finest meal for the lowest fare: Elvio's Pizza. It's the closest to real pizza you'll find anywhere around. They also have calzones, a salad bar and other sandwiches and Italian entrées like stuffed shells, spaghetti and meatballs, and lasagna, all in large portions.

Waterville Valley Resort

WATERVILLE VALLEY, NEW HAMPSHIRE

Waterville is back—with a return to prominence that signifies that the dark days of neglect of the early 1990s are long gone. Since acquiring Waterville in 1996, ski-resort conglomerate Booth Creek has poured millions of dollars into improved lifts, snowmaking and grooming. What hasn't changed is that, with the exception of two intimidating bump runs, this is an ego-boosting mountain covered with good intermediate cruisers that cater to novice skiers and families. To keep families entertained, Waterville has a slew of well-planned programs that keep kids from getting bored and encourage families to play together throughout the day. Activities centered in Town Square include cross-country skiing, snowshoeing, sleigh rides and indoor ice skating. You get all of this at family-friendly prices, which may be why one *SKI* Magazine reader calls Waterville the "best value around the East Coast." But as another reader pointed out, Waterville's proximity to Boston "means big crowds on weekends." Savvy skiers, however, know that lifts open at 8 A.M. and rarely see lines before 10. Another caveat: Waterville's parking is "awful." Late risers should take the shuttle from Town Square or use the valet parking service.

VITAL STATS

SUMMIT: 4,004 feet

VERTICAL DROP: 2,020 feet

SKIABLE ACRES: 255

BEGINNER: 20%

INTERMEDIATE: 60%

ADVANCED/EXPERT: 20%

SNOWMAKING: 100% coverage

AVG. ANNUAL SNOWFALL: 150 in.

LIFTS: 12; 2 high-speed quads, 2 detachable quads, 2 triples, 3 doubles, 4 surface lifts

TERRAIN PARKS/HALFPIPES: 3 terrain parks, 2 halfpipes

INFO: 800-468-2553; www.waterville.com

NEW HAMPSHIRE

SKIING IT

Waterville has a respectable 2,020-foot vertical drop laced with 52 trails. Although it boasts 12 lifts, four of those are surface lifts, and another is a double chair for beginners. Don't despair, though: With Waterville's two high-speed quads, you can make enough runs in the morning to spend the afternoon exploring the valley.

Begin by meeting Quadzilla, Waterville's brightly painted and nattily attired high-speed quad. This is a lift with personality—and a shining example of how the resort courts families. Quadzilla greets arriving skiers with a wide smile, licking his lips in anticipation of the day to come and sporting a red and white baseball cap to shield his sunshine-yellow eyes. Quadzilla is a favorite with kids—be prepared to shell out for a T-shirt—and services lower-intermediate terrain. Valley Run, a wide, smooth cruiser, runs beneath it. Also here are the Wicked Ditch of the East, a snowboard halfpipe; a scaled-down terrain park; and a section of training bumps for mogul-bashers.

Cruising terrain is Waterville's hallmark, making the resort a pleasure palace for intermediate skiers. But it wasn't always so. Upgraded snowmaking (coverage is now 100 percent) and grooming have transformed the once icy mountain into a veritable fabric store: Skiers choose from velvet, corduroy, silk, or satin.

If you want a challenge, take the White Peak Express, which accesses all of Waterville's lifts and terrain. To skier's left, groomed highways such as Periphery, Old Tecumseh and Tippecanoe And Tyler Too ebb and flow with the mountain's contours. The Northside double chairlift, slow but reliable, lets you ski the top of most trails without going all the way to the bottom—a smart move on crowded days. Below the Northside double is Waterville's advanced terrain park, the Boneyard. To skier's right, Oblivion, another blue-square cruiser with one intimidating hairpin turn near the top, hugs the boundary of the ski area.

In between Oblivion and the quad, the Sunnyside triple, which shares the same peak as the quad, serves up Waterville's toughest terrain. Here you'll find a pair of knees-in-your-throat bump runs: Lower Bobby's Run and True Grit, the latter a real trophy trail.

Prefer steep without the bumps? Try Ciao or Gema, both wide fall-line runs that are ideal for carving long-radius turns on shaped skis.

Need a breather? Head to the true summit. It's a long, slow ride on the double chair for a short run. But on warm, sunny days, it's worth it for the view alone. The White Mountain National Forest spreads out below, and Town Square, with its surrounding homes, is dwarfed by the panorama.

FAMILY MATTERS

Waterville is all about families. In fact, their main focus this century is making the place as kid friendly as possible. There's the already mentioned Quadzilla, and the Snowball's Den is a base lodge scaled down to kid size. Little tables, little chairs, and even little restrooms greet little skiers in a fun way. Snowball the Tiger, Waterville's mascot, is always

Hidden in a remote valley in the White Mountain National Forest, Waterville Valley is covered with good intermediate cruisers.

NEW HAMPSHIRE

ready to ski a run, hug a kid, or do something amusing out on the slopes. Even the rental shop—Top Dog Rentals—is in on the fun. Its front door is shaped like a giant doghouse. Kids walk through and are greeted by walls plastered with posters of animals skiing—most of them with helmets on, a good message to get across.

Then there are the programs. Waterville's ski school is renowned for turning kids into great skiers. It's been churning out future champions since its creation in 1966. For tiny ones, the daycare program accommodates children aged six months to four years. Full- and half-day ski and snowboard lessons are available for children from three to 12 years. For little boarders there's even a mini snowboard park with tiny hits.

 **GETTING THERE**
From Boston
Take I-93 North to Exit 28. Take Route 49 to Waterville Valley Resort.
Drive Time: 2 hours

From New York City
Take I-95 to I-91 to I-84 to the Massachusetts Turnpike (I-90). Take I-90 to I-290 to I-495. Take I-93 North to Exit 28. Follow Route 49 to Waterville Valley Resort.
Drive Time: 6 hours

LODGING

Waterville Valley has its own self-contained village, a short, free shuttle ride from the slopes. All bookings can be made through Waterville's central reservations (800-468-2553), or online at www.waterville.com.

Town Square Condos
Waterville Valley, New Hampshire

Located in the heart of the village, these condos offer convenience and ample space for families. The three-bedroom, two-bath units feature fully equipped kitchens, large living/dining areas, cable TVs and VCRs. Units can accommodate up to eight people and are just steps away from all the village action.

The Valley Inn
Waterville Valley, New Hampshire

For a more luxurious stay, The Valley Inn is Waterville's only full-service, four-season hotel. Rooms include master, townhouse and parlor suites which have sitting areas, wet bars, small refrigerators and whirlpool baths. Other amenities include a year-round indoor/outdoor pool, a game room, sauna and Jacuzzi. Breakfast and dinner are served daily, and a meal plan is available. A free shuttle accesses the slopes and Town Square.

The Black Bear Lodge
Waterville Valley New Hampshire

This all-suite hotel is made up of one-bedroom condos that comfortably sleep four to six people. Units feature fully equipped kitchens, dining/living areas, full baths, separate bedrooms and cable TVs. The lodge also has an indoor/outdoor pool, sauna, steam room, whirlpool, children's cinema and game room.

Golden Eagle Lodge
Waterville Valley, New Hampshire

This all-suite lodge has modern-condo amenities and the feel of bygone-era hotels. Units are one- or two-bedroom condos with full kitchens, living/dining areas, full baths, separate bedrooms and cable TVs. The lodge also offers an indoor pool, game room, sauna and whirlpool.

 DINING
Schwendi Hutte
Waterville Valley, New Hampshire

Located just below the summit, this spot takes on-mountain cuisine to new heights. Favorites include Daphne's lobster bisque, large gourmet sandwiches with dips, innovative salads and sinful deserts. Info: 603-236-8330 (x3144)

The Valley Inn
Waterville Valley, New Hampshire

If you feel like dressing up a bit après, this is your choice. The formal atmosphere includes fine linens and candlelit tables. Popular dishes range from seafood to steak to pasta. The best known is the steak Horatio (twin tournedos of beef sautéed with wild mushrooms and smothered in a port, cognac and heavy cream sauce). For a local taste, try the duckling with maple sauce and cranberry-pecan fritter. Info: 603-236-8336

Lattitudes Cafe
Waterville Valley, New Hampshire

Right the middle of Town Square, chef Michael Lambrecht masterminds this newer Waterville dining choice. The setting is soft and comfortable, with twinkling lights and muted colors. Menu items include seafood chowder, New York Strip, Boston baked beans and other regional American fare. Wednesday night's Italian feast is a local favorite. Info: 603-236-4646

Old Waterville Valley Pizza Company
Waterville Valley, New Hampshire

Pizza, pastas, salads, hot and cold subs, soups and hamburgers all done the basic, downhome way. A good choice for a simple night of relaxed eating. Info: 603-236-3663

EVENTS
Canned Food Drive and Toys for Tots
Bring in four cans of food or a new, unwrapped toy worth at least $5 and receive a discounted lift ticket. An affordable and socially conscious way to start the season. Held in December.

NEW HAMPSHIRE

Waterville Valley's 400-foot Superpipe is accessed by the Poma lift.

Jack Williams Ski Race for Wednesday's Child

This fundraiser for special-needs children features WBZ news anchor Jack Williams. A race, auction and celebrity hobnobbing combine for a fun event. Held in March.

April Fool's Ski for a Buck

It's no joke. The deal goes down on April 1 if it falls between Monday and Friday.

 INSIDER TIPS

1) Lifts without lines: North side double or Sunnyside triple.

2) Lifts to take to follow the sun: Start on the North side, move to the White Peak quad, and then onto Sunnyside triple.

3) What to read to find coupons and deals: *Ski Week*.

4) Snow stashes: High Country, Ciao, Gema and Psyched are typically holding the hidden snow.

5) Parking secret: It may be $15, but you can't beat the service of the valet parking. Otherwise, Lot 6. It's directly on your left when you're about to make the sweeping "right turn only" turn, so be careful.

6) Finest meal for the lowest fare: About 10 miles outside of Waterville Valley, the Mad River Tavern is your best bet. It's got a great atmosphere, an extensive menu, and locals love it.

THE BEST OF THE REST OF NORTH NEW HAMPSHIRE

North Conway, New Hampshire

They call it, in medical parlance, "dissociative disease"—multiple personality disorder, in which the patient wears many faces. North Conway, New Hampshire, is like that. It's home to Mt. Cranmore, and close to Wildcat, Black Mountain, King Pine and Attitash Bear Peak ski areas, but the place is foremost a summer town. It's also "the outlet capital of New England." Drive into town and you'll see why: Eighty retail outlets line Route 16—from Anne Klein to Calvin Klein, Geoffrey Beene to L.L. Bean. Dozens of charter buses carrying shoppers from all over the East arrive daily; during fall-foliage season, tourists come from around the world.

But, as former North Conway inn owner Peter Pinkham says, "Appearances deceive. If you looked from the air, you would see that everything on either side of the strip is undeveloped. There are mountains on one side, flood plain on the other." In fact, when you head north past the municipal park in North Conway, it's like leaving Las Vegas and entering Edgartown, Massachusetts.

"There are lots of things to do outdoors here," says Pinkham. "Skiing, golf, hiking, inn-to-inn ski touring, canoeing, fishing, you name it. We're surrounded by 750,000 acres of national forest—so the town is well protected against overdevelopment. We have a dozen movie theaters and all the shopping, yet within three or four minutes there's all that wilderness area."

And there's also the skiing—lots of it. In many ways, North Conway has long offered what so many twenty-first-century mega resorts are trying to attain through master planning and big-time investment: A four-season mountain experience replete with brand-name shopping. The difference is that in North Conway, you get your Anne Klein purse at a discount. —R.N.

NEW HAMPSHIRE

Cranmore Mountain Resort

NORTH CONWAY, NEW HAMPSHIRE

Many skiers scarcely even notice the 192-acre resort that looms behind North Conway's storefronts as they plug slowly along Main Street en route to Black Mountain, Wildcat or Attitash Bear Peak. No matter. Locals are proud to tell you that Mt. Cranmore is still the oldest continually operated ski area in the U.S.

As far as being affordable, where else can you ski in these parts for less than $40 all day, every day, weekends and holidays included? Compare that to weekend lift ticket prices at Attitash Bear Peak or Wildcat, and the savings become even more evident.

This relative value has not gone unnoticed within the ski industry. Les Otten snapped up Cranmore in 1996 during the American Skiing Company's resort-buying rampage. Problem was the U.S. Justice Department felt that ASC's purchase of Attitash, Waterville Valley, and Cranmore—in addition to its ownership of numerous other New England resorts—reeked of trade restraint and ordered ASC to divest itself of Waterville and Cranmore in February 1996.

VITAL STATS

SUMMIT: 1,700 feet

VERTICAL DROP: 1,200 feet

SKIABLE ACRES: 192

BEGINNER: 36%

INTERMEDIATE: 44%

ADVANCED/EXPERT: 26%

SNOWMAKING: 100% coverage

AVG. ANNUAL SNOWFALL: 120 in.

LIFTS: 10; 1 high-speed quad, 1 triple, 3 doubles, 5 surface lifts

TERRAIN PARKS/HALFPIPES: 1 terrain park, 1 halfpipe

INFO: 603-356-5544; www.cranmore.com

Then the White Knight arrived. Booth Creek Holdings' George Gillett, who as owner of Vail in the '80s skyrocketed that resort into industry dominance, took up the gauntlet in the spring of 1996 and went about making Mt. Cranmore better at what it was already good at—providing great skiing for local skiers. Gillett implemented a popular new pricing plan, dropping lift tickets below the previous year's rate of $39. A new Magic Carpet beginner's area, complete with "snow toys" such as snow bikes to help newcomers master carving skills, was also added. Skier visits rose 6 percent to 71,000 in a matter of two years.

The best skiing, if you like it Eastern-gritty, is on the north side, where Austrian legend Hannes Schneider cut the trails by hand. Rattlesnake, Kandahar, Hurricane, Ski Meister and Arlberg are not only a slice of skiing's history, they're bona fide swoopers—wide in spots, narrow in others—and high-octane cruisers that meander, zig and zag with challenges from beginning to end. The lower mountain's south side is primarily beginner terrain, and it's the absolute best most beginners will ever experience, with broad, long and friendly pitches all the way to the bottom. Be sure not to miss the Bandit shortcut back to the base, though, or you'll be faced with an interminable traverse to the quad.

Dividing the north and south sides are Middle Slope and Competition Hill, steep natural racing trails that everyone from the Mountain Meisters to Boston's cops use to settle their bets. For tree skiing, head to Black Forest, Treemeister and Pipeline for bona fide glades. And if your knees are up to it, take a slide on Koessler, Cranmore's toughest run. It's ungroomed and always moguled, but its south-facing bumps are usually soft.

At the top of the mountain is Meister Hut, where the cozy Tyrolian ambiance will have you convinced that the hut was transplanted from the Arlberg. There are historic photos of Hannes on the job, early snow-packing crews, and Red "Hot Rod" Holmes' amazing vintage 1940s grooming machine.

The combination of good-old-days nostalgia and the new full-steam-ahead ownership makes for a unique ski experience that is at once intriguing and welcoming. –D.N.

 GETTING THERE
From Portland

Take Route 302 West to Route 16 South to North Conway. Turn right at the light onto Kearsarge Street and follow signs to Cranmore Mountain Resort.

Drive Time: 1.5 hours

From Boston

Take I-93 North to I-95 North to Spaulding Turnpike/ Route 16 North to North Conway. Turn right at light onto Kearsarge Street and follow signs to Cranmore Mountain Resort.

Drive Time: 3 hours

LODGING
Cranmore Trailside Condominiums
North Conway, New Hampshire

Located adjacent to Lower Kandahar trail, Cranmore Trailside Condominiums offer ski-in–ski-out convenience. Exact layouts vary, but

Cranmore is the oldest, continually operated ski area in the U.S.

with full kitchens and baths, living/dining areas, fireplaces and outdoor decks, they're a great choice for families. Admission to the Cranmore Family Fitness Center is included in any lodging package. Info: 800-SUN-N-SKI

The Cabernet Inn
Intervale, New Hampshire

Located minutes from Cranmore Mountain, The Cabernet Inn's eleven individually decorated guestrooms offer skiers a warm and elegant sanctuary after a day on the slopes. Built in 1842, this completely refurbished cottage features queen beds, private baths, and air conditioning. Choose a room with a fireplace or a Jacuzzi for two, or both. A sumptuous country breakfast, complete with farm-fresh eggs, pancakes and bacon, is served daily. Info: 800-866-4704

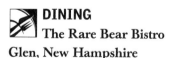

DINING
The Rare Bear Bistro
Glen, New Hampshire

Located in the historic Bernerhof Inn, The Rare Bear Bistro's distinctive menu features traditional old-world Swiss and German classics as well as seasonal delights including duck, handpicked mountain mushrooms and fresh seafood. Be sure to save room for one of The Rare Bear Bistro's decadent deserts—the strawberry cheesecake alone is worth the trip. Info: 800-548-8007

EVENTS
Mountain Meister Series

The Mountain Meister race series attracts over 800 skiers and riders of all abilities each and every week of the 10-week competition. The excitement of the largest weekly citizens-supported downhill ski race series in the U.S. begins the first week of January and concludes in mid-March. Info: 603-356-8540

Black Mountain

JACKSON, NEW HAMPSHIRE

You wouldn't guess by looking at it, but Black Mountain in Jackson, New Hampshire, is the site of some serious firsts. It all started back in 1936, when Jackson was mostly a farming town, skiing was mostly a hike-up affair, and Black Mountain was just some sheep meadows behind a farmer's inn. Then a man named Carroll Reed, who would go on to create a dynasty of schools and shops bearing his name, talked the people of Jackson into a novel concept—opening a ski school staffed entirely by Austrians. Together they created what would become an enduring model for American ski instruction, the first ever Hannes Schneider Ski School in the United States. And just as Reed predicted, people came and the sport grew.

VITAL STATS

SUMMIT: 3,303 feet
VERTICAL DROP: 1,100 feet
SKIABLE ACRES: 143
BEGINNER: 34%
INTERMEDIATE: 33%
ADVANCED/EXPERT: 33%
SNOWMAKING: 98% coverage
AVG. ANNUAL SNOWFALL: 120 in.
LIFTS: 4; 1 triple, 1 double, 2 surface lifts
TERRAIN PARKS/HALFPIPES: 2 terrain parks, 1 halfpipe
INFO: 603-383-4490; www. blackmt.com

That same year, Bill and Betty Whitney, who owned the inn and land that would become Black Mountain, installed the first overhead cable lift in the country and replaced the ropes that dangled from it—and had a nasty habit of getting caught in the bull wheel—with 75 shovel handles from Sears. In 1958, after some disastrous snow seasons, the Whitneys and their partners installed a snowmaking system.

But Black today doesn't look like a history museum; it looks like a pretty typical ski area. Those who have never skied here might dismiss it as a small family mountain. They'd be only half right. Black is laid-back and family friendly, no question, with cheap tickets and cafeteria prices that border on charity. And because the trail system converges at a centralized base area, parents can sit on a sunny deck and watch their kids whiz by.

But Black's size can be surprising. From the parking lot it might look like an overgrown hill-top orchard, but it has 1,100 feet of vertical, and enough twisty, narrow little bump runs to tire the muscles of most expert skiers. While intermediates and beginners are the mountain's bread and butter, Upper Maple Slalom, for instance, winds off the upper chair, past views of the Presidentials, over bumps and twists, and through a hardwood forest that will test any skier's mettle.

Black Mountain is unusual for one other reason: It faces smack-dab southward. Wisdom has it that this is bad for maintaining snow, but Black boasts 98 percent snowmaking coverage and doesn't try to extend the season beyond March. So what it really means is that on those brutally cold days of early January, when every other mountain is warning against frostbite, the folks at Black bake happily in the sun. –N.R.

GETTING THERE
From Portland

Take Route 302 West to Route 16 North to Route 16B. Follow signs to Black Mountain.

Drive Time: 1.5 hours

From Boston

Take I-95 North to the Spaulding Turnpike/ Route 16 to Route 16B. Follow signs to Black Mountain.

Drive Time: 2.5 hours

LODGING
Whitney's
Jackson, New Hampshire

Whitney's is at the base of the mountain. It's a nice family place, and, obviously, you can't beat the access. Info: 603-383-8916

The Christmas Farm Inn
Jackson, New Hampshire

Only a mile down the street from the ski area, the Christmas

Farm Inn offers a nice mix of upscale elegance and backcountry charm. Info: 603-383-4313, 800-HI-ELVES; www.christmasfarminn.com

Don't miss: Breakfast at Yesterday's in Jackson Village; après at the Shovel Handle at Black and the Wildcat Tavern in Jackson Village; dinner at Thompson House in Jackson Village.

Wildcat Mountain

JACKSON, NEW HAMPSHIRE

Wildcat's ascension into the upper echelon of Eastern resorts is like the restoration of a classic Jaguar. The irreplaceable qualities of the past are still there: the jaw-dropping views of the Presidential Range; the narrow, snaking trails designed when skiers hiked up to ski down; the low-glitz, shut-up-and-ski attitude. But now that Wildcat has had a major tune-up, its engine is revving stronger than ever. Whereas a few years ago you endured two poky chairs to reach the 4,062-foot peak, now a high-speed quad whisks you base-to-top in about seven minutes. From the summit, Top Cat and Lift Lion will test your knees and your nerves.

Wildcat isn't for everyone. It offers too much challenging terrain for some, and because it faces Mount Washington (where scientists once clocked the highest wind speed on Earth), it can be downright frigid. But Wildcat can also be blessed with a foot of fluff when its neighbors get rain. "The Colorado of the East," a *SKI* Magazine reader claims. Because it's located in a national forest, Wildcat has been slow to build on-mountain lodging and may never host a swinging nightlife. As one *SKI* reader complains, "You won't find anything but skiing here." But one skier's poison is another skier's pastry: "The people who ski Wildcat are here to ski."

VITAL STATS

SUMMIT: 4,062 feet
VERTICAL DROP: 2,112 feet
SKIABLE ACRES: 225
BEGINNER: 25%
INTERMEDIATE: 45%
ADVANCED/EXPERT: 30%
SNOWMAKING: 90% coverage
AVG. ANNUAL SNOWFALL: 200 in.
LIFTS: 4; 1 quad, 3 triples
TERRAIN PARKS/HALFPIPES: 1 terrain park, 1 halfpipe
INFO: 800-255-6439; www.skiwildcat.com

NEW HAMPSHIRE

Wildcat skiers enjoy views of Mount Washington and the Presidential Range.

 GETTING THERE
From Portland

Take Route 302 West to Route 16 North to Pinkham Notch. Follow signs to Wildcat Mountain.

Drive Time: 2 hours

From Boston

Take I-95 North to the Spaulding Turnpike/ Route 16 North. Follow signs to Wildcat Mountain.

Drive Time: 3 hours

 LODGING
The Town and Country Motor Inn
Gorham, New Hampshire

The Town and Country offers ski and stay packages and is only 15 minutes from Wildcat. Info: 800-325-4386

 DINING
The Wentworth
Jackson, New Hampshire

Located fifteen minutes from Wildcat Mountain, the Wentworth offers fine dining for those who feel like dressing up a bit après ski. Start with the Grilled and Chilled Quail and for dinner try the Herb Crusted Australian Rack of Lamb. Info: 800-637-0013

EVENTS
WFNX Radio Station Après Ski Party

How about skiing or riding to your favorite tunes? WFNX radio station will spin tunes and give away some great prizes. Held in January. Info: 800-255-6439

New England Telemark Festival

Telemark skiers love spring at Wildcat. Come free your heel, learn to telemark or improve on all your skills. Held in March. Info: 800-255-6439

The Balsams

DIXVILLE NOTCH, NEW HAMPSHIRE

Farther north from the Mount Washington Valley, The Balsams operates somewhat like a cruise ship. Virtually everything, from breakfast and dinner to lift tickets and childcare, is included in the price. Meals are lavish, and a large recreation staff fills the days with craft projects, Monopoly games, nature walks and lectures. But it's also better than a cruise ship: The Balsams can't sink, and if it did you'd be surrounded not by open ocean, but by 76 kilometers of cross-country ski trails, a 1,000-vertical-foot ski hill and 15,000 acres of unspoiled forest.

The Balsams takes your breath away. Approaching Dixville Notch, minutes from the Quebec border, you seem to be driving almost vertically, surrounded by sheer cliffs. The setting is reminiscent of the mountain pass where Professor Moriarty allegedly offed Mr. Holmes. Then comes a roller-coaster drop, and a postcard view: stucco Rhineland Renaissance towers and red roofs pinkened in the setting sun beside a mountain lake. And since all of it is surrounded not by condos or second homes or convenience stores, but by miles of spruce, birch and fir, it truly deserves to call itself The Balsams Wilderness.

At The Balsams you'll find not only a team of eager bellmen, but anti-

VITAL STATS

SUMMIT: 2,760 feet
VERTICAL DROP: 1,000 feet
SKIABLE ACRES: 90
BEGINNER: 25%
INTERMEDIATE: 50%
ADVANCED/EXPERT: 25%
SNOWMAKING: 80% coverage
AVG. ANNUAL SNOWFALL: 250 in.
LIFTS: 4; 2 triples, 2 surface lifts
TERRAIN PARKS/HALFPIPES:
1 terrain park, 1 halfpipe
INFO: 800-255-0600;
www.thebalsams.com

NEW HAMPSHIRE

macassars embroidered with The Balsams' three-tree logo on the over-stuffed armchairs; perhaps a woman stretched out on a sofa by a fire reading a book; and Christmas trees in the various common rooms. The Balsams is comfortable, like an old English country home, but not snooty. There are framed Gary Larson cartoons in the bathroom and a ski-waxing station in the lobby.

By the early 1960s, interest in grand hotels had declined to the point where co-owner Warren Pearson observed that The Balsams attracted only two types of guest: "the newly wed and the nearly dead." But a younger, more active clientele began to arrive when the owners built a private ski area nearby in 1966. The mountain, located about one-and-a-half miles away on Wilderness Ridge, doesn't seem to have changed much since it was built, and therein lies much of its charm. Its 16 trails won't challenge the hotshots (though Sunday River, Maine, an hour away, will), and the old chairlift would make all the vice presidents at Mega-Resorts Ltd. cringe.

At The Balsams, you have the same "wait team" at every meal—for decades if you so desire. Never too slick, never too busy, a black-coated group serves up potage of leek, potato and bacon; a cassoulet of scallops, shrimp and lobster; a spinach salad; and a tray of tortes.

On the slopes, The Balsams Wilderness ski area serves up 15 miles of trails and 1,000 vertical feet of skiing from a 2,700-foot summit. There are two triple chairs and two surface lifts. Snowmaking covers 80 percent of the terrain, which is about 50 percent intermediate. One need not be a guest of the hotel to visit the ski slope. —N.R.

GETTING THERE
From Portland

Take the Maine Turnpike (I-495) North to Exit 11. Take Route 26 to Dixville Notch and The Balsams.

Drive Time: 2 hours

From Boston

Take I-93 North to Exit 35. Take Route 3 to Route 26 East to Dixville Notch and The Balsams.

Drive Time: 3.5 hours

THE BEST OF THE REST OF SOUTH NEW HAMPSHIRE

Ragged Mountain Resort

DANBURY, NEW HAMPSHIRE

The folks at Ragged have managed to strike a near-perfect balance between the old and the new, leaving out only what you don't really need. Absent is the glitz and pomp of so many master-planned resorts—a look that often resembles a space ship that has crash-landed in a cow field in rural America. Not at Ragged; it's comfortably at home with its surroundings. A steep-roofed, green-and-white classic New Hampshire design is repeated throughout the resort, from lift buildings to storage shacks. In addition to the throwback architecture, you'll find that Ragged also runs a number of throwback chairlifts. These beautifully maintained fixed-grip diesels give the mountain historical continuity, while their modest uphill capacity helps keep skier density down on the Spear Mountain Peak area.

But it's not all anachronism here. A stone's throw from Spear Mountain's fixed-grip triple lurks the state's only high-speed detachable six-pack. It accesses Ragged's 2,250-foot summit, where you'll find spectacular views of the snowcapped Presidential Range, Cardigan Mountain to the north, and Kearsarge Mountain to the south.

VITAL STATS

SUMMIT: 2,250 feet
VERTICAL DROP: 1,250 feet
SKIABLE ACRES: 220
BEGINNER: 30%
INTERMEDIATE: 40%
ADVANCED/EXPERT: 30%
SNOWMAKING: 90% coverage
AVG. ANNUAL SNOWFALL: 100 in.
LIFTS: 9; 1 high-speed six-pack, 2 doubles, 2 triples, 4 surface lifts
TERRAIN PARKS/HALFPIPES: 1 terrain park, 1 half-pipe
INFO: 603-768-3600; www.ragged-mt.com

NEW HAMPSHIRE

For its size, the mountain offers are a nice mix of challenge and family-friendliness. From the top of the six-pack, you can funnel onto blue cruisers (Lower Ridge, Lower Chute, Northeast Territory), go under the chair and take Exhibition (blue) to Birches (black), or head right and speed onto the nicely groomed Sweepstakes (black). Beginners will find a couple easy-to-locate greens that take them all the way to the lodge.

Ragged's best-kept secret is Spook's Gorge. The resort recently carved the five new glades into the ravine that lies between Ragged's two main peaks. It's where you'll find Joe's Ravine, arguably Ragged's toughest trail. Accessed off the left of the Spear triple, Joe's is a tight, twisting ride over

Ragged Mountain Resort maintains classic New Hampshire designs at its family-friendly facilities.

steep pine-studded ledges. At the bottom of the steeps, the pines give way to a wide-open hardwood glade that gently nurses you back to the slopes.

 ## GETTING THERE
From Boston

Take I-93 North to Exit 17. Take Route 4 West to Route 104 East. Turn right at Ragged Mountain Road.

Drive Time: 2 hours

 ## LODGING
Ragged Mountain Condominiums
Danbury, New Hampshire

Located five minutes from the resort, the Ragged Mountain Condominiums feature two bedrooms, kitchenette, cooking utensils, dining area, cable TV, VCR, phone and basic linens. Ski-and-stay packages are available. Info: 800-400-3911

Ridgeline Cabin
Danbury, New Hampshire

Want to step out the door in the morning, click into your bindings and cut fresh tracks without having to ride the chair? Perched atop Ragged Mountain's Northeast Peak, the Ridgeline Cabin offers the ultimate in "on mountain" lodging. The only one of its kind in New England, this 2,000-square-foot log cabin can accommodate up to 30 people. The cabin's remote location is accessible only by chair lift or snow cat. Amenities include wood stove, bunk beds, cooking facilities, full bath and an authentic New England outhouse. Info: 800-400-3911

DINING
The Pasquaney Restaurant & Wild Hare Tavern
Bridgewater, New Hampshire

The Pasquaney Restaurant & Wild Hare Tavern is renowned for its delicious cuisine, but the view of Newfound Lake from the dining room is the real treat. Fiercely protected by the locals, the lake is one of New Hampshire's most beloved secrets, and consequently, one of the cleanest lakes in the East. Depending on the season, try and get a table on the veranda at sunset—it promises to be a meal you won't forget. Info: 603-744-9111

EVENTS
Ragged Mountain Downhill

One of the few races of its kind left in existence. Get the long boards out of the garage and get yourself to Ragged Mountain for a chance to break the 70 MPH mark. Held in March.

Eastern Boarder's "Last Call"

A one-of-a-kind event with a jam sessions format and a knock out system. Crowd judging and lots of interaction make this an event not to be missed. Red Bull after party in the Pitchfork Pub. Held at end of season.

Mount Sunapee Resort
NEWBURY, NEW HAMPSHIRE

What happens when a neglected, state-run ski area is leased to the husband-wife team already credited with turning around Okemo Mountain in Vermont? Another turnaround. Mount Sunapee's new caretakers have invested millions in on-mountain improvements. There's the new post-and-beam base lodge, a 950-vertical-foot trail (Lynx), and increased snow-making, which now covers 97 percent of the trail network. *SKI* Magazine readers noticed. "New management has made a huge difference in the quality of snow and friendliness of the staff," remarks one *SKI* reader. Even

NEW HAMPSHIRE

Wildcat skiers enjoy views of Mount Washington and the Presidential Range.

Sunapee's Sunbowl, New Hampshire's only lift-accessed back bowl, enjoys new popularity with visitors eager to use the new quad to reach its wide-open terrain. "Skis like a big mountain (for New England, that is), with medium-mountain prices," comments another *SKI* reader. The mountain features two areas—North Peak and South Peak—plus a snowboard area, with South Peak catering specifically to beginners. Nostalgic Sunapee skiers should note that some things haven't changed—like the summit warming hut's gigantic stone fireplace or the stunning view of Lake Sunapee as you drop into Sunbowl on Upper Wingding. Also stubborn to change are the large number of skiers on some of Sunapee's narrow, 50s-style trails. Says one *SKI* reader: "There are too many blue squares and too many people on one slope." But what Sunapee lacks in expert terrain, it makes up for with long, serpentine cruises. Try skiing midweek for zero liftlines and empty hill space. If you haven't been to Mt. Sunapee since its facelift, it might be worth a visit.

VITAL STATS

SUMMIT: 2,743 feet

VERTICAL DROP: 1,510 feet

SKIABLE ACRES: 220

BEGINNER: 40%

INTERMEDIATE: 50%

ADVANCED: 10%

SNOWMAKING: 97% coverage

AVG. ANNUAL SNOWFALL: 150 in.

LIFTS: 10; 3 quads, 2 triples, 1 double, and 4 surface lifts

TERRAIN PARKS/HALFPIPES: 1 terrain park, 1 halfpipe

INFO: 603-763-2356; www.mtsunapee.com

NEW HAMPSHIRE

GETTING THERE
From Boston

Take I-93 North to I-89 North to Exit 9. Take Route 103 West to the Mount Sunapee traffic circle.

Drive Time: 1.5 hours

NEW HAMPSHIRE

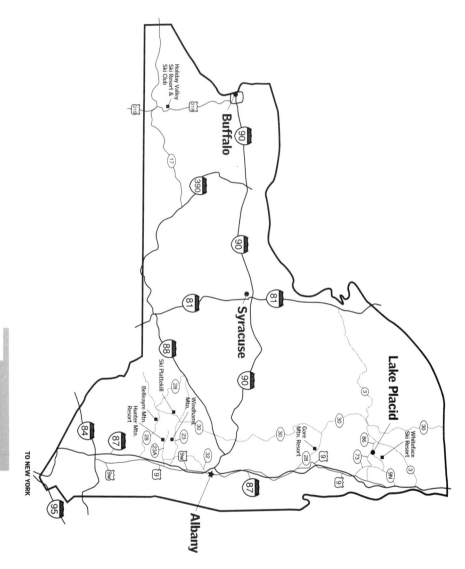

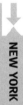

NEW YORK

New York

SKI MAGAZINE'S GUIDE TO NEW ENGLAND AND QUEBEC

Whiteface Ski Resort

WILMINGTON, NEW YORK

Despite the fact that it was the skiing venue for the 1980 Lake Placid Winter Olympics, most Eastern skiers remain clueless as to how good Whiteface really is. How else to explain it hosting as few as 150,000 skiers during a recent epic winter? (On the positive side, that can leave the hill empty a lot of the time.) For the uninformed, let's dispel two popular misconceptions. Misconception number one: Whiteface is too tough and too cold. Reality: In 2001, reversing two decades of post-Olympic neglect, the New York State Legislature began reinvesting in this state-owned resort. Snowmaking and grooming arsenals were pumped up, and trails were recontoured to provide desperately needed intermediate routes off the summit. That same year, the big missing piece of the puzzle was put in place: the heated, eight-passenger Cloudsplitter gondola, which soars to the top of Little Whiteface peak. Misconception number two: Beginners have no place here. Reality: Whiteface has become a great place to learn to ski. Its Direct to Parallel program, which makes use of ultra-short skis, has had great success. Convinced you should give Whiteface a try? If not, here's the kicker: Lake Placid is just 10 miles away, and it's the East's most vibrant mountain town (sorry, Stowe). You're hard-pressed to find a better winter vacation spot in the East.

VITAL STATS

SUMMIT: 4,867 feet

VERTICAL DROP: 3,430 feet

SKIABLE ACRES: 220

BEGINNER: 20%

INTERMEDIATE: 36%

ADVANCED/EXPERT: 44%

SNOWMAKING: 97% coverage

AVG. ANNUAL SNOWFALL: 168 in.

LIFTS: 10; 1 high-speed gondola, one 8-pasenger heated gondola, 1 high-speed quad, 1 fixed quad, 1 triple, 5 doubles

TERRAIN PARKS/HALFPIPES: 1 terrain park, 1 halfpipe

INFO: 518-946-2223; www.whiteface.com

NEW YORK

SKIING IT

Whiteface (the peak), the one you see when you pull into the main parking lot, is knee-shakingly steep, enough of a challenge for any skier to walk away satisfied—if not terrified. But Whiteface (the resort) is not steep all over. The ski area is comprised of three summits: Little Whiteface, which is a haven for intermediates and cruisers; Easy Acres, an all-beginner

Whiteface boasts the longest continuous vertical in the East.

peak unto itself; and the aforementioned Whiteface Peak.

The best way to start out at Whiteface is to jump in the heated gondola and head to the top of Little Whiteface. From there, ski a few long cruisers. With 2,400 vertical on that peak alone, there's plenty of time to carve before you catch a lift again. You can go smooth and easy with Excelsior, a three-mile cruise with nice views, or start out with the thigh-burning Approach. Upper Parkway, site of the 1980 Olympic giant slalom, is another superb cruiser. The run starts fast and steep then flattens out a bit as it switches to intermediate on Lower Parkway. If one run isn't enough, a quick turn around the trees takes you to the Freeway lift (Chair 7). The double chair gives you a short breather before dropping you at the top of the run to do it again.

If you're craving bumps, take on Wilderness, where the World Cup mogul run is set. If it's ungroomed you like, hit Empire on Little Whiteface. About the width of a Volkswagen Beetle, it is never groomed—simply because snowcats won't fit on the trail. On a good snow day, it's a place to feel like you're in the backcountry without leaving lift-accessed areas.

When you're ready for the big time, head to Whiteface Peak, where only experts are advised to go. The runs are steep, long and often narrow and challenging in that uniquely New England way.

For the real thrill seekers, check out the Slides area, which opens after big snows. It's thirty-five acres of ungroomed backcountry, accessed by the Summit quad and a short hike. Cliffs and other typical backcountry obstacles exist, so skiing in pairs is a good idea. Don't take it lightly.

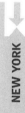

NEW YORK

Beginners will want to spend all of their time at Easy Acres, a peak unto itself where all the trails are well-groomed, gentle and forgiving. There's enough variety to help a beginner make the next step, too. And the lack of advanced skiers flying through at high speeds allows for a comfort level that's often hard to find.

FAMILY MATTERS

Easy Acres is what it's all about when it comes to families at Whiteface. The self-contained mountain within a mountain has its own rental shop, ski-school area, restaurant, and parking. Kids can be dropped off at 8 A.M. here—a great bonus for parents who love to make first tracks. The Bunny Hutch Nursery is also found here, as are the kids' ski programs, including Play and Ski for four-to six-year-olds, which combines a day-care setting with some time out on the mountain. While Whiteface's kids' area is a separate mountain, it is easy to access. Parents wanting to swing by and check on the young ones need only take one cruiser down, pop in, and then catch a lift back up.

The Whiteface Junior Adventure program is for kids seven to 12, and kids as young as three can take private lessons. For teens, the Whiteface Teen Experience is a ski school that's more like spending a day at a ski camp. Teens are grouped by ability and brought out on the mountain for a full day of challenges.

GETTING THERE
From Montreal

Take Route 15 South to I-87 South to Exit 34. Take Route 9 North to Route 86 to Whiteface Mountain.

Drive Time: 2 hours

From New York City

Take the New York State Thruway (I-87) North to the Adirondack Northway (Exit 24). Take Exit 30 to Route 9 North to Route 73. Continue on Route 73 to Lake Placid. Take Route 86 East to Whiteface Mountain.

Drive Time: 5 hours

From Boston

Take the Massachusetts Turnpike (I-90) to Albany. Take I-787 North to Route 7 West to I-87 North. Take Exit 30 to Route 9 North to Route 73. Continue on

NEW YORK

Route 73 to Lake Placid. Take Route 86 East to Whiteface Mountain.
Drive Time: 5 hours

From Buffalo
Take I-90 East to Exit 36. Take I-81 North to Route 3 East to Saranac
Lake. Take Route 86 East to Whiteface Mountain.
Drive Time: 5.5 hours

LODGING
There is no slopeside lodging at Whiteface. And while that sacrifices
convenience, it gives the ski area an unusual development-free aesthetic.
There's a free shuttle from just about every hotel and lodge in the greater
Whiteface/Lake Placid area, and the action at night is in the town anyway.

Ledge Rock at Whiteface
Wilmington, New York
Directly facing Whiteface Mountain, with well-appointed American
hotel rooms, this is the only choice for those who want to walk to the lifts.
It has basic amenities, with some kitchenette rooms available. Children
under 18 stay free. Info: 800-336-4754; www.ledgerockatwhiteface.com

Mirror Lake Inn
Lake Placid, New York
Located about 10 miles from Whiteface, the Mirror Lake Inn is a traditional inn with all the amenities of a modern resort lodge. Warm
mahogany walls, polished walnut floors, marble and stone fireplaces,
antiques and chandeliers provide a cozy atmosphere and understated
elegance. Rooms and suites are available. The onsite health spa features
massages and other body treatments as well as a cardiovascular exercise
room with views of the lake. Other amenities include a restaurant, cocktail
lounge, spa, indoor pool, hot tub/Jacuzzi and some rooms with fireplaces.
Info: 518-523-2544; www.mirrorlakeinn.com

The Lodge at Lake Placid
Lake Placid, New York
If you're traveling without the kids, take a tip from Robert Redford,
who booked The Lodge for the millennium, or Bill Gates, who stayed
there regularly until the baby came along. Conceived as a comparatively

NEW YORK

Host to the 1932 and 1980 Winter Games, Whiteface maintains its Olympic heritage with state-of-the-art wintersports facilities.

proletarian alternative to its sister property, The Point (where rarefied rooms start at $1,000 a night), The Lodge is a far cry from spartan.

Handcrafted log beds are cushioned in down and rooms are warmed by massive stone fireplaces; fresh cookies await bedside. Of the 37 rooms (some tucked into the original 1882 lodge), the cabins are most interesting—especially the Whitney, with its preponderance of red-and-black plaid offset by zebra-print accents which reads like an Adirondack-style safari camp. Fifteen miles of cross-country trails unfurl outside the door and, across Mirror Lake, Whiteface hulks expectantly. Info: 518-523-2700; www.lakeplacidlodge.com

DINING
Brown Dog Deli & Wine Bar
Lake Placid, New York

Funky decor, an eclectic menu, and a wine list that seems a mile long—that's what brings crowds to the Brown Dog, named after the owner's three chocolate labs, who are often out front to greet you. Info: 518-523-3036

Interlaken Lodge & Restaurant
Lake Placid, New York

Once a classic, and reopened in 2002, the Interlaken is the spot for an elegant meal. Located in the Adirondack Victorian Inn in the heart of Lake Placid, this family-owned-and-operated inn offers friendly service and wonderful cuisine. Specialties include rack of lamb with rosemary-cabernet sauce, fresh fish and black-angus filet mignon. Info: 518-523-3180; www.innbrook.com

 EVENTS
World Cup Events

The Olympics were held here twice, and world-class events still come to the mountain. Check Whiteface's website for the season's calendar, which usually include a World Cup freestyle event, a bobsled competition and Nordic ski jumping.

INSIDER TIPS

1) Lifts without lines: The good news here is, with under 200,000 skier visits a year, there's almost never a big crowd at Whiteface. Still, insiders know to take the gondola to Little White Face and cruise that area in relative solitude.

2) Runs to take to follow the sun: From the summit ride Skyward into Lower Cloud Spin. From there, dip into Lower Valley, hit Easy Street briefly and hop back onto Lower Valley.

3) What to read to find coupons and deals: Your best bet is the resort website, www.whiteface.com.

4) Snow stashes: For high-level skiers, the Slides. For others, the Little Whiteface Glades.

5) Parking secret: None. But the shuttles run fast, frequent and free. They're your best bet.

6) Finest meal for the lowest fare: Nicolas Over Main. Greek-influenced American fare that is served past 10 P.M.—great for late-night munchies.

Hunter Mountain Resort

HUNTER, NEW YORK

Since the early days of the Industrial Revolution, when leisure time was an embryonic ideal, the Catskill Mountains have been a vacation haven for New York City's working class. And although the Catskills' summer tourist fortunes have drooped during the past two decades, its major ski areas continue to draw snow-hungry City dwellers in winter. None captures the New York spirit more than Hunter Mountain. Though it may not quite be the "Snowmaking Capital of the World" that it calls itself, Hunter does do a splendid job of both snowmaking and grooming. The area keeps the snow guns pumping at every opportunity through most of the season, and with the right conditions Hunter can turn a rain-soaked or sloppy mountain into a winter wonderland overnight. That said, the Hunter region will never be mistaken for Stowe, Vermont, or North Conway, New Hampshire. Hunter and its lodging and entertainment base, the town of Tannersville, lack the charm of the former and the commercial bustle of the latter.

VITAL STATS

SUMMIT: 3,200 feet

VERTICAL DROP: 1,600 feet

SKIABLE ACRES: 240

BEGINNER: 29%

INTERMEDIATE: 29%

ADVANCED/EXPERT: 42%

SNOWMAKING: 100% coverage

AVG. ANNUAL SNOWFALL: 125 in.

LIFTS: 11; 3 quads, 2 triples, 5 doubles, 1 surface lift

TERRAIN PARKS/HALFPIPES: 1 terrain park, 2 halfpipes

INFO: 888-HUNTERMTN; www.huntermtn.com

Skiing, however, is why most folks head to Hunter. The lure of close-to-home, big-mountain skiing keeps skiers flocking here, especially on weekends. While other resorts might offer better amenities, Hunter delivers pure skiing close to New York City—with 1,600 feet of often gnarly vertical, it's no Berkshire bump.

SKIING IT

This is a New Yorker's ski area—the pace is as fast and furious as Grand Central Station. Be prepared to compete for everything from a locker to a parking space. A school bus shuttles skiers from the outer reaches of the parking lot, but savvy regulars who miss the close-in spots head to the Hunter One beginner area and jump on the C-lift to reach

NEW YORK

the main mountain lifts. (Note: Lift tickets are sold at the Hunter One area on weekends only.)

If you need to store gear in the main lodge and don't want to lug it from the lot, a drop-off area is next to the lodge. Remember to lock up your stuff or ask a friend to watch over it. Good skis have a tendency to grow legs at Hunter.

When ticket lines become long, use the cash-only or Guest Services windows on the side of the base lodge. Few people know you can purchase tickets there, so lines are usually nonexistent.

Hunter's SKIwee and MiniRider programs for kids are housed in a separate building to the left of the lodge. Be sure to make reservations and arrive early: The scene can resemble a Wizard of Oz munchkin reunion. On peak days, the programs reach capacity, and if you're not registered by 9:15 A.M., your child's spot may be given away.

If you haven't had breakfast, grab a cup of java and some of the cafeteria's freshly baked coffee cakes–they put Drake's to shame.

Beginners and low intermediates should turn left out the front door of the base lodge and head to Hunter One. Better still, sign up for a beginner ski or snowboard lesson and start the day with some game improvement. The beginner ski package gives you access to all lower mountain trails and lifts, including Hunter's new Broadway Limited and 20th Century Limited fixed-grip quads. H-lift, at the area's far left boundary, is usually empty and is a great place for learners to practice their skills on busy days.

The AA-lift (everyone just calls it "the quad") is dead center in front of the base lodge and functions as the expressway to the top. Intermediates and above should take the quad to the summit and snake their way around the mountaintop to Hellgate. Don't let the name scare you; during early morning hours, the wide, sunny trail to mid station is excellent. By noon, the crowds have usually skied off the good snow, and Hellgate grows bumps that make it live up to its moniker. Experts may opt instead for The Cliff, a tighter but parallel alternative to Hellgate. From mid station, cruise down Seventh Avenue onto Gun Hill Road (hey, this is a ski area for New Yorkers) and head back up.

Skiers looking for a less challenging warm-up will enjoy Belt Parkway, like its namesake city highway a meandering cruise that runs back to the base. Essentially a ledge trail carved from the shoulder of Hunter's rocky flanks, it gets little sun and tends to glaze up earlier than other trails. So get your fill early.

NEW YORK

Hunter's Snowtubing Park features twelve 1,000-foot chutes and three tube tows.

After 10 A.M., the queue at the quad grows long. Hunter West, an expert-only area, is usually open by now and better skiers should head there and stay off the main mountain. Even though Hunter West is served by two older double chairs, you'll probably get in more skiing. Intermediates usually shy away from West because of its reputation, but Way Out, a relatively gentle expert run, feeds down to the West lifts. You can then ride up and look to see if you can handle West's testy main trails.

If not, find the Heuga Express trail, a wide, well-groomed cruiser that dumps out below the mid station. This is a great trail for advanced intermediates and experts because the access is somewhat hidden, which means the run isn't as well traveled as the rest of the mountain's front side. —K.M.

FAMILY MATTERS

Around the late 1990s, the Hunter brass realized they needed to spruce up the ski area's family offerings. And spruce them up they did. Today, the Learning Center at Hunter Mountain (opened in December 2001) is a model of a family-friendly learning environment, with a building that was constructed expressly to simplify the beginner experience. Inside are the Ski and Snowboard School, the children's programs, the PlayCare facility, a ticket-sales counter, a rental shop, Goldye's Cafe and a retail shop.

One of the reasons parents love the Learning Center is because they can sit fireside in Goldye's Cafe and watch their kids on the slopes outside.

For aspiring snowboarders, Hunter Mountain is one of five Burton

Learn-to-Ride Kids Method Centers in the U.S. Beginner packages, children's programs and private lessons all make use of the Center's equipment and expertise.

For families who love speed, the NASTAR race park provides timed fun for the whole gang. Certified coaching, video analysis and race-park season passes are available are all parts of the program. It's a great alternative to the Hunter Mountain Competition teams, which include junior racing, snowboarding and freestyle.

GETTING THERE
From Albany
Take the New York Thruway (I-87) South to Exit 21. Take Route 9W South to Route 23A West. Follow to Hunter Mountain.

Drive Time: 1 hour

From New York City
Take the New York Thruway (I-87) North to Exit 20. Take Route 32 North to Route 32A North to Route 23A West. Follow to Hunter Mountain.

Drive Time: 2.5 hours

From Boston
Take the Massachusetts Turnpike (I-90) West to Albany. Take the New York Thruway (I-87) South to Exit 21. Take Route 9W South to Route 23A West. Follow to Hunter Mountain.

Drive Time: 3.5 hours

From Philadelphia
Take I-76 to I-95 East to I-287 North. Take the New York Thruway (I-87) North to Exit 20. Take Route 32 North to Route 32A North to Route 23A West. Follow to Hunter Mountain.

Drive Time: 4 hours

LODGING
Hunter Mountain has its own lodging reservations service (888-HUNTER-MTN) which books area hotels, motels, B&Bs, as well as lift-side condominiums. The resort has been upgrading lodging choices recently. Better options include:

Hunter Inn
Hunter, New York

Among the most expensive choices, the Hunter Inn is elegant and comfortable. But don't let your budget scare you away: There are great ski-and-stay packages that make the luxury more affordable. Plus, the Inn is located near the mountain's base, something worth extra cash on a ski trip. All bookings include a hearty buffet breakfast. A cozy guest living room located adjacent to the lobby has an oversized TV and a Sony Playstation. The rec room, located on the lower level, offers a variety of video games, ping-pong, air hockey and foosball. The Inn also has a pool and exercise room. Info: 518-263-3777; www.hunterinn.com

Villa Vosilla
Tannersville, New York

For a good family choice, try Villa Vosilla, a resort with a real Italian feel. The Villa offers special ski-and-stay packages, and family-style dinners—all included in the package price. Amenities include a beautiful indoor heated spa, complete with pool, Jacuzzi, saunas, steam bath, exercise room, game room and four stone fireplaces. Info: 518-589-5060; www.villavosilla.com

Liftside Village at Hunter Mountain
Hunter, New York

The real luxury here is the ski-to-your-door location. For folks looking to spend most of their time doing on-mountain activities, this is the choice. Each unit has a fireplace, slopeside deck, cable TV and VCR, and washer and dryer. Info: 888-HUNTER-MTN, www.huntermtn.com/reserve.htm

DINING
Bear Creek Landing
Hunter, New York

Something for everyone in the family: Fireside dining with a spectacular view of the mountain, a private ice rink, and cuisine ranging from Wasabi tuna and sashimi to steaks, seafood, pasta, chicken and vegetarian dishes. Kids can eat staples like charbroiled burgers and wraps, and then head to an arcade room. Open for lunch and dinner. Info: 518-263-3839; www.bearcreeklanding.com

Hunter's extensive snowmaking and fleet of snowcats can turn a rain-soaked mountain into a winter wonderland overnight.

Pancho Villa's
Tannersville, New York

With quick service, homemade chips and salsa, a kids' menu and Cadillac Margaritas, locals call Pancho's the best-kept secret in Tannersville. Top-notch Mexican entrées with prices almost too good to be true don't hurt its reputation, either. Info: 518-589-5134

EVENTS
Hunter Mountain Racing Foundation Snow Ball and Fireworks, New Year's Eve

The Racing Foundation Snow Ball is an annual event open to the public. Tickets are on sale throughout December, and the proceeds benefit Hunter Mountain's Racing Foundation, which actively supports up-and-coming racers. Live music, a silent auction, one hour of open bar, and a dinner round out the event's lineup.

Annual FDNY and East Coast Firefighter's races

The New York Fire Department has held races at Hunter Mountain for over 30 years. The weekday festivities include racing, dining and drinking, as the Northeast's bravest meet in the Catskills to celebrate the spirit of brotherhood. Held in early February.

Heineken/Amstel Torchlight Parade and Fireworks

The annual fireworks display lights up the night and the torchlight

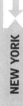

NEW YORK

parade sees hundreds of skiers wielding torches as they wind down Hunter's slopes. The breathtaking spectacle is open to the public to enjoy. Held Presidents' weekend.

U.S. Para-Ski Championships

"Para" as in parachute. This event combines a helicopter, jumpers, and a ski race, and the unusual mix makes for a fantastic weekend. On Saturday, skydivers attempt to land on a five-square-meter target. Sunday's events include a Giant Slalom race, and participants are scored in both events with winners moving on to compete internationally. Held in late March.

Annual Pond Skimming and Beach Bash

Skimmers don outrageous costumes and attempt to cross a giant frozen pool of water to score points with the judges. The pond skimming is just one part of the season-closing beach party, which also includes live music, barbeque, and, of course, the last ski opportunity of the season. Held in mid April.

INSIDER TIPS

1) Lifts without lines: If you are a good skier or rider, you can avoid the lines at the high-speed Snowlite Express quad by riding F lift from mid mountain and skiing the east side.

2) Lifts to take to follow the sun: The sun hits the east side early, so take the quad to the summit and ski Hellgate while the powder is fresh from the previous night's snowmaking. The west side of the mountain opens at 9:30 A.M., and the sun gets there around noon. Hit the moguls when they soften up in the afternoon and beat the lines at the mountain's base by riding the West Side's two dedicated lifts, Z and Y.

3) What to read to find coupons and deals: *The Hunter-Windham Scene* or *The Catskill Country*.

4) Snow stashes: Clair's Way hoards powder days after a storm, but the real secret is Annapurna. Most people are too scared to venture in that direction, and it's among the longest and steepest on the hill. Locals also head to K-27 for nasty bumps and powder in excess.

NEW YORK

5) Parking secret: A paid-parking area next to the Learning Center is cheap and convenient, but it fills up fast. The real rock-star parking is part of the new High Peaks Club Locker membership. Members of the club get their own reserved parking area at the lodge's west wing. It's the way to go if you visit often. In general, the early bird gets the parking spot.

6) Finest meal for the lowest fare: The Sushi Bar at Hunter Mountain. It's unique, and has a great selection and atmosphere—and the convenience of being right inside the main lodge. It's authentic sushi at fair rates—a great find in the mountains. Also, Jerry's deli in the base lodge has the best wraps, salads, and soups in town. Although the price seems high, the quality is outstanding.

Windham Mountain
WINDHAM, NEW YORK

When urban refugees want to treat themselves well, they head to Windham, where the abundance of spiffy new SUVs makes the parking area look like a dealer lot. Located in the northern belt of Catskill resorts, Windham is just over two hours by car from New York City—in Rip Van Winkle territory, where the names of the creeks and rivers feeding the Hudson end with "kill," and the fading signs of pre–Jet Age tourist splendor sit alongside similarly well-worn mill and mountain towns. Windham was founded as a private club for city escapees during the Catskills' pre-war heyday. Today it is smack in the middle of gracious second-home land. Its motto: "The Cure for the Common Life." Think of the ski area, then, as the tidy family Victorian—albeit one with a slopeside business center offering everything from on-mountain paging to secretarial services—located next to the rambunctious frat house. —C.S.

VITAL STATS

SUMMIT: 3,100 feet
VERTICAL DROP: 1,600 feet
SKIABLE ACRES: 262
BEGINNER: 30%
INTERMEDIATE: 45%
ADVANCED/EXPERT: 25%
SNOWMAKING: 97% coverage
AVG. ANNUAL SNOWFALL: 110 in.
LIFTS: 7; 1 quad, 4 triples, 1 double and 1 surface lift
TERRAIN PARKS/HALFPIPES: 1 terrain park, 2 halfpipes
INFO: 800-754-9463; www.skiwindham.com

NEW YORK

SKIING IT

All the usual caveats of Eastern resorts apply at Windham. Its summit elevation is 3,100 feet, with a 1,600-foot vertical drop—not bad, but not big-mountain skiing. And you can't trust the friendly skies to provide an all-season base. Conditions can change in a day, requiring the resort to blow snow on 97 percent of its terrain. This is not such bad news, since resorts that depend on snowmaking invariably offer better snow than those that don't.

Caveats aside, the resort's twin summits offer a terrific variety of terrain. The less trafficked eastern hill is dominated by three long, challenging expert runs—Why Not, Wing 'N It and Wicked—and a boundary-hugging beginner run, Wanderer, which provides the best view of the surrounding countryside. To the west, the main mountain runs the gamut from intermediate cruisers to the brutal double-diamonds Wipeout, Wedel and the encouragingly named Wheelchair. (Yes, all the names of Windham's runs begin with a "W," which makes it hard to sound macho as you suggest, Gilbert and Sullivan–style, a descent from Wraparound and Whisper to Warpath and Wiseacre.)

Crowds tend to keep to the Whirlwind quad serving the main mountain, leaving the parallel Whistler triple almost unused. From the summit, the best runs (especially Warpath and Wiseacre) are broad avenues that do a good job bearing heavy traffic of various ages and skill levels.

Farther west, while lines might still be long at the quad, there is usually no waiting at the Wheelchair lift, which serves the westernmost, mainly expert runs. From the top, good skiers will find themselves returning to Upper and Lower Wolverine, a perfectly paced run that plunges from the summit through medium-sized moguls before leveling off into a delightful wide avenue that empties out at the base lodge. The real treat: This classy run is often almost empty—the snow-sliding equivalent of finding no one on Fifth Avenue on a summer Saturday. —C.S.

FAMILY MATTERS

Like all good resorts in the know, Windham has an area dedicated to kids and learning. It's called the Children's Learning Center (CLC) and it's stocked with specially designed equipment and staffed with well-trained instructors. The simple lessons and all-day programs are all designed not only to help a child learn to ski but to make some friends, too. All participants (ski or snowboard) are grouped by age and skill level for half day (A.M.) or full-day sessions. Small classes and "Kids Only" terrain provide a confidence-inspiring atmosphere to learn in. The CLC is also home to indoor programs for non-skiing children. Theme days, puppet shows and games are offered all-day, half-day, or hourly. Mountain Masters, a program designed for older children, caters to ages eight to 12.

GETTING THERE
From New York City
Take the New York Thruway (I-87) to Exit 21. Take Route 23 West to Windham Ski Area.

Drive Time: 2.5 hours

From Boston
Take the Massachusetts Turnpike (I-90) to Albany. Take the New York Thruway (I-87) to Exit 21. Take Route 23 West to Windham Ski Area.

Drive Time: 3.5 hours

LODGING
Windham Arms
Windham, New York

Windham operates the recently refurbished Windham Arms, which features spacious rooms and a number of amenities that will appeal to families, including a skating rink in the rear. The hotel also offers a restaurant, game room, movie theater, fitness center, fireplace, bar and lounge. A free shuttle to and from the mountain runs all day—and until night skiing ends. Ski-and-stay packages as well as kids-stay-free packages are available. Info: 518-734-3000

Albergo Allegria
Windham, New York

Just one mile from the ski area, this 21-room Victorian mansion was built circa 1892. Suites with Jacuzzis and fireplaces are available, and the Albergo offers a hardy gourmet breakfast and a homey but elegant feel. Info: 518-734-5560, www.albergousa.com

NEW YORK

INSIDER TIPS

1) Lifts without lines: On busy weekends or holidays, skip the high-speed quad and hit the F Lift. For upper-level skiers and riders, B Lift now serves advanced and expert terrain, and typically has low traffic.

2) Lifts to take to follow the sun: Start on the East Peak using B Lift, C Lift, A Lift, or F Lift to access the eastern most trails. As the sun moves to the center of the mountain, stick with A or F and then head to the West Peak and G Lift in the afternoon.

3) What to read to find coupons and deals: Check out the Entertainment coupon book for discounts, and visit the Bargain Shopper page on the Windham website regularly. The very best and latest deals are always there.

4) Snow stashes: On weekends and holidays, make a reservation for a First Tracks tour, which start before the lifts open.

5) Secret parking: It's no secret, but the valet parking gets you to the front door for $14.

6) Finest meal for the lowest fare: It's hard to beat Vines Bistro (at the Windham Arms Hotel) for quality. The prices are very reasonable for such excellent food. Brandywine Restaurant's Pasta Night is also an excellent value.

Belleayre Mountain
HIGHMOUNT, NEW YORK

Located two-and-a-half hours outside New York City in the Catskill Forest Preserve, Belleayre Mountain is a welcome departure from the hustle and bustle of the city, not to mention its neighboring resorts. Where other Catskill ski areas cater to the SUVs and nightlife, Belleayre's peaks remain unblemished by the glare of commercialization and overcrowding. Sans glitz and glamour, this is the place for old fashioned, uncrowded and unpretentious skiing.

NEW YORK

SKIING IT

Belleayre's trails descend through the silent, serene woodland of the preserve, declared "Forever Wild" by New York State in 1885. The pristine terrain at this state-operated resort caters mostly to beginner and intermediate skiers with a smattering of advanced trails at the top of the mountain.

Novices should head to the Discovery Lodge where long beginner runs and a top-notch ski school welcome their arrival. Roaring Brook and Iroquois are gentle cruisers perfect for recent graduates. Beginners feeling a little more adventurous can make tracks to Deer Run, a long and winding intermediate trail on the west end of the mountain.

Until recently, the main complaint from experienced Belleayre skiers revolved around the length of its advanced trails and the separation between the lower and upper mountain. The resort has remedied the situation, connecting the mountain with a quad chair running from the Discover Lodge to the summit, lengthening trails and adding two new advanced trails, including the 1000-vertical-foot Dot Nebel (named for the Belleayre trail designer and race coach). Two new groomers and 60 new tower guns complete the resort's overhaul, enhancing grooming and snowmaking capabilities.

VITAL STATS

SUMMIT: 3,325 feet
VERTICAL DROP: 1,404 feet
SKIABLE ACRES: 193
BEGINNER: 28%
INTERMEDIATE: 62%
ADVANCED/ EXPERT: 10%
SNOWMAKING: 96% coverage
AVG. ANNUAL SNOWFALL: 116 in.
LIFTS: 8; 2 quads, 1 triple, 2 doubles, 3 surface lifts
TERRAIN PARKS/ HALFPIPES: 1 terrain park, 1 halfpipe
INFO: 845-254-5600; www.belleayre.com

FAMILY MATTERS

Parents of young Belleayre skiers and snowboarders breathe easier knowing the uncrowded beginners' area is completely separate from the intermediate and advanced areas. This ensures those wrong turns onto advanced runs and kamikaze teens will not ruin the learning process. The resort also offers a SKIwee/MINIrider Program with low student to instructor ratios and a dedicated staff.

For youngsters not yet ready to hit the slopes, Belleayre's nursery is equipped with everything children 1 to 6 years old need to have fun while their parents enjoy the mountain. −A.P.

NEW YORK

GETTING THERE
From New York City
Take the New York Thruway (I-87) to Exit 19. Take Route 28 West to Highmount and Belleayre Mountain.

Drive Time: 2.5 hours

LODGING
Alpine Osteria Bed and Breakfast
Highmount, New York

The Alpine Osteria Bed and Breakfast offers skiers a cozy room less than a quarter-mile from Belleayre Mountain. Located on 37 private acres in the Catskill Mountains, the Alpine Osteria offers a full breakfast in the morning, a warm fireside after a day on the slopes and a family-friendly atmosphere. Amenities include Jacuzzi whirlpool baths, fireplaces, double-headed showers and king size beds. Info: 845-254-9851

Birchcreek Inn
Pine Hill, New York

The Birchcreek Inn is a turn-of-the-century inn located on 23 acres a half-mile from Belleayre Mountain. Amenities include daily fireside breakfast, vintage billiard room, spacious library and cable TV. Ask about discount ski and dinning packages and children rates. Info: 845-254-5222

DINING
Pine Hill Arms Restaurant
Pine Hills, New York

A Catskill Mountain Landmark for over 120 years, the Pine Hill Arms Restaurant offers two dining rooms and an exceptional menu. Dine in the traditional Catskill Mountain Room with rustic barnwood siding or the Greenhouse Room with sensational views of the range. Specialties include fresh seafood, grilled steaks and prime rib. Try the country style breakfast for a meal to energize you for a day on the slopes. Info: 800-932-2446.

THE BEST OF THE REST OF NEW YORK

Holiday Valley Ski Resort and Holimont Ski Club

ELLICOTTVILLE, NEW YORK

With little fanfare, Holiday Valley draws upwards of 450,000 skiers each winter, making it New York's busiest ski resort. While it doesn't stretch high—it sports a 750-vertical-foot rise—it ranges wide, with three distinct base areas dotting its winding access road. Nearby Holimont—the largest private ski area in the country in terms of members—has similar vertical, but it doesn't spread as far.

The culture at both areas is clubby but unpretentious, a unique blend of egalitarian and elitism that rarely exists in skiing today. Both have dominant groups of regulars, most prominently at Holimont, where opening weekend brings 1,240 families from Western New York, Ontario and Ohio together like a giant college reunion. Holimont even owns a patent on a popular snowmaking gun (thanks to a group of members who helped develop it) and receives up to $50,000 in royalty payments annually to help defray expenses.

While Holiday Valley is decidedly more commercial, it too has a strong scent of skiing as it used to be. The Ellicottville Ski Club, which traces its roots to the 1930s, has its own clubhouse at the base of the lifts. Enter its vestibule and you'll be greeted by a grid

VITAL STATS

HOLIDAY VALLEY
SUMMIT: 2,250 feet
VERTICAL DROP: 750 feet
SKIABLE ACRES: 266
BEGINNER: 35%
INTERMEDIATE: 27%
ADVANCED/EXPERT: 38%
SNOWMAKING: 95% coverage
AVG. ANNUAL SNOWFALL: 180 in.
LIFTS: 12; 2 high-speed quads, 7 quads, 1 double, 2 surface lifts
TERRAIN PARKS/HALFPIPES: 3 terrain parks, 2 halfpipes
INFO: 716-699-2345; www.holidayvalley.com

VITAL STATS

HOLIMONT VALLEY
SUMMIT: 2,250 feet
VERTICAL DROP: 725 feet
SKIABLE ACRES: 135
BEGINNER: 25%
INTERMEDIATE: 25%
ADVANCED/ EXPERT: 50%
SNOWMAKING: 95% coverage
AVG. ANNUAL SNOWFALL: 180 in.
LIFTS: 8; 2 quads, 2 triples, 3 doubles, 1 surface lift
TERRAIN PARKS/ HALFPIPES: 1 terrain park, 1 halfpipe
INFO: 716-699-2320; www.holimont.com

NEW YORK

Holiday Valley's 52 slopes extend over 1,1100 acres.

of cubbyholes filled with wicker picnic baskets, the more elaborate ones emblazoned with family crests in ski motifs.

In Holiday Valley's Tannenbaum lodge, an elegant riverstone and log-timber complex patterned after Vail's Two Elk Lodge, the top floor is one of the classiest brown-bag areas of any ski resort. Some families bring the trappings of home, decorating the tables with floral cloths and coolers filled with beer and wine. In a bow to local tradition, the perimeter is ringed with numerous electrical outlets, so the regulars can plant themselves at a table and plug in their Crock-Pots filled with home-cooked meals. It all amounts to a hominess you can see and feel—and sometimes smell.

GETTING THERE - HOLIDAY VALLEY
From Buffalo

Take I-90 West to Exit 55. Take Route 219 South to Holiday Valley. Drive Time: 1 hour

From Pittsburgh

Take Route 119 North to Route 219 North to Holiday Valley. Drive Time: 3.5 hours

Thirty-nine trails are open for night skiing at Holiday Valley.

GETTING THERE - HOLIMONT
From Buffalo

Take I-90 West to Exit 55. Take Route 219 South to Ellicotville. Take Route 242 West to Holimont.

Drive Time: 1 hour

From Pittsburgh

Take Route 119 North to Route 219 North to Ellicottville. Take Route 242 West to Holimont.

Drive Time: 3 hours

Don't miss: A sleigh ride over the slopes that even a budget-conscious family can enjoy, Mansfield Coach and Cutter of Little Valley, New York, provides a classic red sleigh pulled by an enormous black Percheron, Molly the "Gentle Giant." There's room for up to six people and the ride lasts about 15 minutes. The cost is exceptionally reasonable, and infants and toddlers are free. Rides are available in the afternoons during Christmas week, December 26 to January 1, and then Saturday afternoons for the rest of the season, depending on the weather.

LODGING

Holiday Valley offers lodging right on the slopes. The Inn at Holiday Valley is at the base of the Sunrise lift for ski-in—ski-out stays. Rooms are spacious and comfortably decorated. The Inn has an

NEW YORK

indoor/outdoor pool, hot tub, sauna and massage therapy. A continental breakfast is served daily, and complimentary shuttle service is available to the Main Chalet. Info: 716-699-2345

 DINING
The Ellicottville Brewing Company
Monroe Street, Ellicottville

Award-winning menu, microbrews and great architecture—what more could you want? Try the Coconut Shrimp or the beer-batter seafood special. Info: 716-699-ALES

Gore Mountain Resort

NORTH CREEK, NEW YORK

Owned by a state government notorious for bloated bureaucracies, Gore Mountain is one tax-supported operation that actually works. The hill is deceptive, with most of its respectable 2,100 vertical feet hidden behind a false summit. The terrain tends to meander, dip, and roll in an older, narrower style—by legal decree. The state's constitution actually limits ski trail width in the Adirondack State Park. Experts rip it up under the Straight Brook Chair and on the area's signature steep run, Rumor. The Gore gondola is warm, old and slow. It takes about 20 minutes to reach the summit and the weekend queues are long; it's best to stick to the chairs. Despite the nearby town of North Creek, which has ski history dating back to the 1930s, it's a sleepy place with few services or amenities. Most overnight skiers stay about half an hour away in Lake George. The Sagamore, about 10 minutes closer, is a spectacularly restored grand hotel set on a peninsula. The Sunday brunch will make you late for the slopes.

VITAL STATS

SUMMIT: 3,600 feet
VERTICAL DROP: 2,100 feet
SKIABLE ACRES: 300
BEGINNER: 10%
INTERMEDIATE: 60%
ADVANCED/EXPERT: 30%
SNOWMAKING: 95% coverage
AVG. ANNUAL SNOWFALL: 150 in.
LIFTS: 11; one 8-passenger gondola, 2 quads, 2 triples, 3 doubles, 3 surface lifts
TERRAIN PARKS/HALFPIPES: 1 terrain park, 1 halfpipe
INFO: 518-251-2411; www.goremountain.com

NEW YORK

Gore's 2,100-foot vertical is hidden behind a false summit.

GETTING THERE
From New York City

Take the New York Thruway (I-87) North to Exit 23 (Warrensburg). Take Route 9 to Route 28 to Peaceful Valley Road.

Drive Time: 4.5 hours

Ski Plattekill

ROXBURY, NEW YORK

As mom-and-pop ski-area owners go, Laszlo and Danielle Vajtay—like the ski area they own—defy stereotypes. Sure, they run their area as a bootstraps-up, self-financed small business, but Ski Plattekill is no kiddie hill. Laszlo was 32 when he chucked a successful corporate career in his native New Jersey and bought the area at a 1993 bankruptcy auction. He had learned to ski here at age 7, become the area's youngest instructor at 16, and met his wife here in 1985, when Danielle's family were regulars from Connecticut and Laszlo was the dashing ski-school director. Now they work 18-hour days to survive in the shadow of regional giants Hunter and Belleayre.

The Vajtays bill Plattekill as a family ski area, but the kind of families that would be most comfortable here might be the Mahres, McKinneys and Moes. Sure, there are a couple of extra-long beginner runs. But it's the genuine 1,000 feet of continuously tilted, twisted, old-time vertical that

NEW YORK

Former New Jersey businessman Rick Laszlo has owned Ski Plattekill since 1993.

makes Plattekill a must-visit for serious skiers.

And Laszlo exhibits a skier's heart. While the area is normally open Friday through Sunday and holidays, he spins the T-bar on "Powder Daize," any weekday when snowfall tops 12 inches. That happens more than you'd think: On the western fringe of the Catskills, the area can suck down more than 200 inches of lake effect in a good year. That'll get you eight Powder Daize.

The Vajtays have upgraded snowmaking to ensure good conditions. But the kitty is a bit short to execute their dream of replacing the workhorse T-bar that services the black-diamond-studded North Face. They've already bought the chair, and the liftline has been cut, adding 100 vertical. "We just need the financing to buy towers and do the install," Laszlo says. "So if you know anybody out there who wants to own part of a true gem, tell them to call," he says. That's 607-326-3500, folks. "My extension is 8," Laszlo adds. —S.C.

VITAL STATS

SUMMIT: 3,500 feet

VERTICAL DROP: 1,100 feet

SKIABLE ACRES: 600

BEGINNER: 20%

INTERMEDIATE: 20%

ADVANCED/EXPERT: 40%

SNOWMAKING: 85% coverage

AVG. ANNUAL SNOWFALL: 165 in.

LIFTS: 4; 1 triple, 1 double, 2 surface lifts

TERRAIN PARKS/HALFPIPES: 1 terrain park, no halfpipes

INFO: 607-326-3500; www.plattekill.com

NEW YORK

GETTING THERE
From Albany

Take I-90 West to I-88 West to Exit 23. Take Route 30 South, turn right onto Bridge Street and follow signs to Ski Plattekill.

Drive Time: 1.5 hours

From New York City

Take the New York State Thruway (I-87) North to Exit 19 (Kingston). Take Route 28 West to Route 30 North. Turn left onto Cold Spring Road and follow signs to Ski Plattekill.

Drive Time: 2.5 hours

Kissing Bridge
GLENWOOD, NEW YORK

Plainly visible from downtown Buffalo office windows is all the incentive desk jockeys need to get their work done quickly: Black snow bands, like smoke trailing from coal-fired steam engines, drape across Lake Erie and race into the hills south of town. There's no time to waste. It could be snowing three inches an hour, so you want to beat snarling traffic. If you're efficient, you can get home early from work, throw the boards in the car, spend three hours skiing powder at Kissing Bridge– and still be home in time to watch the third period of the Sabres game with a plate of wings. Western New York isn't a big winter sports destination. But the region is graced with a half-dozen or so distinctive ski areas. Most are day trips or mini-vacations for residents of New York, Ontario, Ohio and Pennsylvania. Kissing Bridge is three and a half hours from Cleveland, four from Pittsburgh. But mostly, it's Buffalo's backyard ski area, where the locals go to play: no condos, no timeshare resorts, no fancy restaurants. Function is favored over Bogner.

VITAL STATS

SUMMIT: 1,715 feet

VERTICAL DROP: 550 feet

SKIABLE ACRES: 760

BEGINNER: 34%

INTERMEDIATE: 33%

ADVANCED/EXPERT: 33%

SNOWMAKING: 98% coverage

AVG. ANNUAL SNOWFALL: 250 in.

LIFTS: 8; 2 quads, 1 triple, 3 doubles, 2 surface lifts

TERRAIN PARKS/HALFPIPES: 1 terrain park, 1 halfpipe

INFO: 716-592-4963; www.kissing-bridge.com

NEW YORK

"We're a day area with personality," says President Mark Halter. "We encourage our employees to play and have fun with our customers. We're not a mall with lifts." And where one Buffalo mall recently banned unescorted teens, Kissing Bridge welcomes them. They're like bad party guests: first to show up, last to leave. "We don't have the mystique of a big mountain, but we make it interesting," says Ray Wozniak, KB's executive vice president in charge of mountain ops. The key is a state-of-the-art terrain park, which Wozniak designed after idea-stealing trips to bigger resorts. This year, the park has been upgraded to accommodate all levels of ability.

But Kissing Bridge's appeal is not limited to freeriders. There are restaurants, on-mountain cafeterias and the aptly named Lake Effect Saloon. There are kids' and beginners' programs, a nursery and a tubing park. Best of all, there are narrow tree-lined trails, wide-open cruisers, and steeps and bumps to keep the adults happy while the kids learn to make turns.

Lights keep the trails open and buzzing until 10:30 P.M. six nights a week. From 9 A.M. to 5 P.M. on weekdays, you'll have the place to yourself. Then the after-school clubs and commuters arrive. For them, there's no place like home. Especially on a powder night. —F.D.

GETTING THERE
From Buffalo

Take I-90 West to Route 219 South. Exit Armor Duells Road to Route 240 South. Follow signs to Kissing Bridge.

Drive Time: .5 hour

From Albany

Take I-90 West To Route 219 South. Exit Armor Duells Road to Route 240 South. Follow signs to Kissing Bridge.

Drive Time: 2 hours

NEW YORK

NEW YORK

Ste.-Agathe-des-Monts

117

15

■ Tremblant

87

15

Montreal

40

10

20

Ski ■
Bromont
Mont Sutton ■
Owl's Head ■

243

55

Quebec

20

91

55

■ Mont Orford

Sherbrooke

Stoneham ■
Mtn. Resort

Mont-Sainte-Anne ■

Le Massif ■

138

St. Lawrence

Quebec

SKI MAGAZINE'S GUIDE TO NEW ENGLAND AND QUEBEC

Tremblant

MONT TREMBLANT, QUEBEC

At some point during your Tremblant vacation, you'll see a small knot of serious people strolling the village taking notes. These are rival ski executives making a pilgrimage (and shaking their heads about their own pitiful villages back home). What comes naturally to Tremblant, other resorts spend millions trying to duplicate: "Europe in North America!" a *SKI* Magazine reader cheers. Human-scale, personable, and quaint without being forced, Tremblant remains the Mona Lisa of ski area villages. It is a joy to walk to the lifts in the morning, stopping for coffee and pâtisseries at one of the many cafes (Au Grain de Cafe, for instance). But smart skiers look to Tremblant for what it can offer: elegant wooded runs that flow like streams down the mountainside. "Hidden trails, surprises—what great fun!" one *SKI* reader says. Check out the tumbling Ryan Haut to Ryan Bas, then the glades found at Versant Soleil (try Bon Vieux Temps, Brasse-Camarade and Les Bouleaux). Accommodations, such as the St. Bernard and the Westin Resort Tremblant, continue to set the gold standard for the industry, earning Tremblant *SKI* Magazine's No. 1 ranking in lodging. Reader complaints read like a Chicago weather report: "Cold, rain, windy," but readers quickly kiss and make up, noting "Tremblant's not at fault." Crêperie Catherine may be the best spot this side of Chamonix for a casual but civilized ski lunch. Famously uncivilized is Le P'Tit Caribou, where clothing becomes increasingly optional as Tremblant's full-throttle nightlife extends into the hours when decent Americans are in bed. For the sixth year running, Tremblant has delivered the whole package to Eastern skiers—superior skiing, service and base village. As one *SKI* reader concludes: "a winter wonderland." And English-speakers need not worry about the language barrier in Quebec. Even if you're not bilingual, most Quebecois at Tremblant are.

VITAL STATS

SUMMIT: 2,871 feet
VERTICAL DROP: 2,116 feet
SKIABLE ACRES: 610
BEGINNER: 17%
INTERMEDIATE: 33%
ADVANCED/EXPERT: 50%
SNOWMAKING: 76% coverage
AVG. ANNUAL SNOWFALL: 150 in.
LIFTS: 13; one 8-passenger gondola, one 6-passenger gondola, 6 quads, 2 triples, 3 surface lifts
TERRAIN PARKS/HALFPIPES: 1 terrain park, 1 halfpipe
INFO: 888-736-5268; www.tremblant.ca

QUEBEC

SKIING IT

Tremblant has had trails on both its north and south sides for decades, but they've added and expanded the terrain to the point where you can now practically ski all 360 degrees. Most of the greens are on the south side (the side facing the village). If you're a beginner or an intermediate in need of a warm-up run or two, take the gondola to the top and try out La Crete, Bon Vivant and Nansen. You can then stick to the TGV lift, a quad that serves the upper half of the mountain, or head back to the bottom for more runs off the gondola.

Anyone looking for a little more challenge should start the day on the sunny side. Tremblant recently added 20 percent more terrain off the eastern side of the mountain, called Versant Soleil. About 10 trails were designed to follow the natural contours of the mountain and are mostly narrow twisters and glades, all served by a high-speed quad, Le Soleil. Take a cruise down Franc-Sud, Toboggan and Tapecul to warm up in the early morning light, then do it again, only this time drop into the glades of Brasse-Camarade or Bon Vieux Temps. If you're a first-tracks fanatic, Tremblant has a weekend program that allows you to take the gondola to the summit for breakfast at the Grand Manitou, then cop freshies at 8 A.M. while the luckless snooze.

The north side catches early light. Take the gondola from the village to the peak, where you can drop down a spread of two dozen trails. To the east (left as you face the north side), you'll find big bumps on black diamonds such as Banzai, Boiling Kettle and Geant.

In the afternoon, stay south. The Gondola will take you to a wide range of trails. Pick from classics such as the Kandahar (named for one of the first and hairiest races in North America) or a narrow black chute called Fripp. The Flying Mile quad on the bottom half tends to attract fewer crowds, and, depending on wind direction, it can be more sheltered and therefore warmer. −N.R.

FAMILY MATTERS

It took less than a decade for Tremblant to develop a colorful base village and crisscross the mountain with an extensive trail network. Now the resort is focusing its energies on family programs. Witness such new on-mountain developments as the addition of two Magic Carpets to the beginner area and a snow-park expansion that includes a baby park for the tiniest skiers. For older children and rank beginners, they've cut Petit

Tremblant's Kidz Club offers daycare, ski lessons and dining steps from the beginner slopes.

Bonheur, a green trail on the north side of the mountain. Tremblant also took a hard look at X-Zone, its adults-only nighttime ski area, and decided that kids rule. So X-Zone is adult-only no more—and now offers tubing on Wednesday and Saturday nights.

The resort's Kidz Club is one of the best kids' facilities anywhere in the country. Located next to the beginner slopes at the base of the mountain and walking distance from anywhere in the village, Kidz Club is daycare, ski lessons and dining for the little ones all rolled into one. Forget their goggles? You can buy a pair here. Rentals? A kids' rental shop is on premises.

As for the Ecole de Neige, it's one of the few bilingual ski schools in North America. So your kids will come off the mountain with "bonjour" and "merci" in their vocabularies as well as some newfound snow skills. Young riders can venture to the new beginner halfpipe in the X-Zone Adventure Park, while their older siblings can take advantage of the half-pipe used for the nationals.

GETTING THERE
From Montreal

Take Route 15 North to Sainte-Agathe. Just past Sainte-Agathe, Route 15 North merges to become Route 117 North. Take Route 117 North to Exit 119. Folow signs to Tremblant.

Drive Time: 1.5 hours

QUEBEC

From Boston

Take I-93 North to I-87 North. At the Canadian border I-87 North becomes Route 15 North. Take Route 15 North to Sainte-Agathe. Just past Sainte-Agathe, Route 15 North merges to become Route 117 North. Take 117 North to Exit 119. Folow signs to Tremblant.

Drive Time: 6.5 hours

 LODGING
Chateau Mont Tremblant
Mont Tremblant, Quebec

Chateau Mont Tremblant is, arguably, the finest hotel—certainly the largest slopeside hotel—in all of Eastern skiing. Inspired by the grand Provençal-style residences that dominated merchant squares throughout the La Belle Provence in the 19th century, the Chateau encompasses just enough of the history and eccentricity to keep you aware that you're in the French-speaking Laurentians. Unlike many newer hotels, it's not a building filled with mundane furnishings and ersatz art. Instead, antiques, stained glass and folk art are everywhere, capturing the look of Old Montreal and its pitched, ribbed rooftops, stucco sidings, fieldstone-covered chimneys and ubiquitous wrought iron. In short, the Chateau is a slice of France, easily accessible from most points East.

Despite the Chateau's imposing exterior, the public spaces are cozy, warm and welcoming—giving you the impression that you've just entered a petite auberge rather than a 316-room hotel. The staff is among the most courteous and attentive in hospitality-dom. The cuisine, imaginatively prepared and magnificently presented, tops expectations by any measure, and the wine list—recognized as one of the most outstanding in the world—could keep a connoisseur content for life.

But no one comes here simply to indulge the palate. It's the skiing that draws most visitors, and with ski-in—ski-out access, you're as close to it as you can get.

All guest rooms include views of the mountain, village and Lac Tremblant. There is also a health center with indoor/outdoor pools, three Jacuzzis, sauna, steam baths, fitness equipment, exercise room and spa. Enjoy a feast at the 156-seat mountain-view Le Windigo Restaurant, or take out lighter fare at Le Wigwam Cafe on terrace level. Info: 819-681-7000; www.fairmont.com –R.N.

QUEBEC

Le Sommet des Neiges
Mont Tremblant, Quebec

This five-star, 120-unit condo-hotel is located about 30 feet from the heated gondola. Guests can mingle by the octagonal stone fireplace, relax in the outdoor Jacuzzi, or work out in the exercise room. All suites feature a fireplace, a fully equipped kitchen, and a washer and dryer. Info: 800-461-8711

The Marriott Residence Inn
Mont Tremblant, Quebec

This more-affordable option is located in the heart of Tremblant's pedestrian village and offers a variety of air-conditioned rooms and suites. All suites (one- and two-bedroom) are equipped with a full kitchen, a fireplace and two televisions. Prices include continental buffet breakfast, indoor parking, snacks during social hour (Monday to Thursday) and access to an exercise room and outdoor heated pool. Info: 888-272-4000

Le Westin Resort Tremblant
Mont Tremblant, Quebec

Le Westin provides comfort, luxury and service in the heart of the pedestrian village. The hotel offers slopeside access, Japanese cuisine from Soto, an outdoor whirlpool, an exercise room, round-the-clock room service and a concierge service. All suites, from a single to a three-bedroom, have a fireplace, kitchenette and deluxe "Heavenly Beds," Westin exclusives. Info: 866-836-3030

 DINING
Aux Truffles
Mont Tremblant, Quebec

Dinner on this continent doesn't get more romantic or rich with foreign flavor than at Aux Truffles. Although the village setting at the base of Tremblant is Old Quebec, the food, created by chef and part owner Pier Cousineau, is creative French. When you hunger for something special, Aux Truffles delivers. The atmosphere is elegant and intimate, without being stuffy; the service is attentive at a leisurely pace.

The five-course menu includes entrées such as rack of caribou with mustard and rosemary sauce, duck breast roasted in balsamic vinegar and served with blueberry confit, and loin of lamb served with almonds and citrus compote. There is always a fish of the day and a chef's choice. As is French custom, a salad or cheese plate is served after the entrée. Foie gras, a house specialty, is well represented on the à la carte menu.

Feeling adventurous? Try the "La Table du Chef Pier," a six-course selection of the chef's specialties. Choose a table near the paned-glass windows to watch the promenade of passers-by or to look out over the lower village. On a wintry night, ask for a fireside table for added warmth and romance. Prices are steep, but worth the splurge, and the Canadian exchange rate provides a sharp discount. Reservations are recommended. Info: 819-681-4544 —H.N.

Le Westin Resort
Soto Restaurant Sushi Bar
Japanese fine dining. Sushi, maki and sashimi and a variety of cooked dishes of meat prepared the Soto way. A don't miss while visiting Tremblant. Info: 819-681-4141

Dining secrets: You pay a premium to eat in Tremblant's village, which nearly eliminates the advantages of the strong dollar. The best luxury food is at La Forge (819-681-4900), which offers creatively prepared local ingredients like Atlantic salmon carpaccio marinated in single-malt scotch and rack of Quebec piglet with honey and shallots. L'Atre du Inn (819-681-3000), in Tremblant's original inn, serves a prix-fixe lunch—pea soup, sauté of chicken breast, salad and coffee. Creperie Catherine (819-681-4888) puts everything into their fresh breakfast crepes, from mixed berries and chocolate to ham and Gruyere.

EVENTS
Grand Prix 24h de Tremblant with Jacques Villeneuve
Held in late December annually, this friendly 24-hour race is open to all skiers and snowboarders who want to have fun and strive to challenge themselves in the name of children. The proceeds from this event go to Juvenile Diabetes Research Foundation.

Ericson Freestyle World Cup
The best in the world gather at Tremblant for aerial and halfpipe competitions. Held during Tremblant's teen week every January.

Molson Ex Pro Challenge

The best snowboarders and freeskiers in the world come together to compete for $35,000 in prize money. Special events and live music surround the competition, which is held in early April.

 INSIDER TIPS

1) Lifts without lines: After taking the gondola to the top, doing laps off the TGV or Soleil lifts is the best way to avoid crowds.

2) Lifts to take to follow the sun: It's simple: Morning means Northside; afternoon means Southside.

3) What to read to find coupons and discounts: *The Tremblant Express.*

4) Snow stashes: The locals are so tight-lipped about the hidden powder that we couldn't find out!

5) Finest meal for the lowest fare: Microbrewery La Diable is a local favorite. They brew beer on-site and serve good meals at a low cost. The pedestrian village has around 30 restaurants at all prices.

Mont-Sainte-Anne
BEAUPRÉ, QUEBEC

Sitting on the eastern border of Quebec is a wonderful ski secret that surprisingly few have gotten wind of. About an hour's drive from Quebec City proper, the Charlevoix region features a handful of ski areas nestled in the Laurentian mountain range. Tucked alongside the wide and breathtaking St. Lawrence River, there are no big cities here, nor are there major destinations in themselves (although Mont-Sainte-Anne can stand up to a vacation on its own). But taken as a whole, the friendly French Canadian way of life, the woodsy feel and the steep mountains that, paired with the river, create a microclimate that practically guarantees a few powder days each week, the Charlevoix region can be a magical destination for winter-sports lovers.

You can stay in Quebec City or at the base of either Stoneham or Mont-Sainte-Anne and explore the two ski areas plus another regional area, Le

Massif, with one multi-day lift pass. Stoneham is a 326-acre ski area with a 1,380-foot vertical set in a horseshoe-shaped valley just 20 minutes north of Quebec City. More than half of the slopes are lit for night skiing, and snowmaking covers 86 percent of the mountain. The bar is a lively place after skiing.

With 428 skiable acres, Mont-Sainte-Anne offers more variety of terrain. Many of the trails are longer here than at Stoneham, and even beginners can explore the entire 2,000 feet of vertical. Better skiers and riders will enjoy the terrain used for women's skiing and snowboarding World Cup events.

Both Stoneham and Mont-Sainte-Anne have covered chairlifts, and Mont-Sainte-Anne has a gondola to combat the northern cold. Both have childcare facilities and children's ski schools.

Mont-Sainte-Anne is easy to figure out. As you face the mountain, the easiest trails are to the right. As you move to the left, they gradually turn very difficult. The most hardcore will want to grab the front (south side) of the mountain early, while it's the least skied out. Warm up on Gros Vallon, then take Traverse to the Triple Chair, which serves the top half of the mountain and the most difficult runs. Test your taste for steeps on the famous S, which has bumps, or Super S, which is groomed. Then try double-black Brunelle, a steep, mogul-strewn glade between Espoir and the chair. Cool down on Montmorency, then stop for lunch at the authentic French creperie next to the gondola for a buckwheat crepe filled with goat cheese and tomatoes or kiwi and chocolate. La Crête, meanwhile, on the leftward-most shoulder, provides spectacular views of the ice-encrusted St. Lawrence River, the Île d'Orleans (a big island mid river) and Quebec City in the distance. No wonder it's the favorite launching site for paragliders, who jump off at the summit and glide along the ridges to the bottom. Wrap up the day by skiing the north side for the sunset. Most of the trails on this side of the mountain are mellow, because there's less vertical. But because it's north facing, it's also the area that opens first and closes last.

VITAL STATS

SUMMIT: 2,625 feet

VERTICAL DROP: 2,050 feet

SKIABLE ACRES: 428

BEGINNER: 23%

INTERMEDIATE: 46%

ADVANCED/EXPERT: 31%

SNOWMAKING: 80% coverage

AVG. ANNUAL SNOWFALL: 160 in.

LIFTS: 13; 1 high-speed gondola, 3 quads, 1 triple, 2 doubles, 6 surface lifts

TERRAIN PARKS/HALFPIPES: 1 terrain park, 2 halfpipes

INFO: 418-827-4561; www.mont-sainte-anne.com

QUEBEC

photo by Jean Sylvain

Skiers stay warm in Mont-Sainte-Anne's two covered lifts and 8-passenger gondola.

GETTING THERE
From Quebec City

Take Highway Montmorency (440) East to Route 138 East. After Beaupré, take Route 360 to Mont-Sainte-Anne.

Drive Time: 1.5 hours

LODGING
Auberge St. Antoine
Quebec City, Quebec

"La Belle et La Bête" is what Mont-Sainte-Anne calls itself. But just 30 minutes from "beauty and the beast," you can luxuriate in the stonewalled comfort of Auberge St. Antoine. This stylish retreat in the heart of the Old Port district of Quebec overlooks the St. Lawrence River. Beamed cathedral ceilings, whitewashed walls, and antiques are what you'll find here. And the city's best bistros are just a few doors away. Info: 888-692-2211

DINING
L'Aventure Beaupré
Beaupré, Quebec

This lively restaurant and disco on Mont-Sainte-Anne's access road packs them in with reasonably priced, eclectic fare and a fun atmosphere. From the combination bar and dining room, you gaze out huge windows as the night-skiing lights wink on at the ski area. Nothing is fancy here: just good family-oriented fare at fair prices (made even more so by the exchange rate). And it's definitely a skier hangout. The vast room is decorated with snow-sport paraphernalia—even a chairlift chair. The menu—you can ask for an English version—is international, with fondues, pastas, nachos, Californian chicken, wood-oven pizzas and even fajitas. But everything manages to have a French accent. Choices go well beyond the usual to include appetizers such as wild game pâté and main dishes such as bow tie pasta and smoked salmon with capers, shallots, white wine, parmesan cheese and cream. You'd be hard pressed not to find something to warm you on a cold winter's night. Info: 418-827-5748 —H.N.

Le Massif

PETITE-RIVIERE-SAINT-FRANCOIS, QUEBEC

Despite being the East's sixth-highest ski area in terms of vertical drop (2,526 feet), Le Massif isn't really a mountain at all. It's an upside-down ski area, tumbling from the edge of the Canadian Shield into the deep channel cut by the massive St. Lawrence River. Skiers park at the top, which means that within minutes of their arrival, they can be skiing. But if it's snowing and it's your first visit, you'll have to take the trail map's word for it that there are ski trails descending into the fog, or that there really is a river down there.

Then, halfway down, the St. Lawrence comes into view, though the eyes need a moment to trust what they're seeing. A crumpled brown-tinged moonscape of broken ice spills across tidal flats to the edge of the water. The far shore, 13 miles away, hides in mist. Midstream, a gargantuan freighter parts the icy water, headed east (right to left) to the Atlantic. At your feet remains another 1,300 feet of winding, forest-lined ski trails. It's big-mountain skiing—with a maritime twist.

Le Massif's upside-down layout and veritable seaside setting are just the start. There's also the overlay of French. Here in Quebec's Charlevoix

VITAL STATS

SUMMIT: 2,645 feet

VERTICAL DROP: 2,526 feet

SKIABLE ACRES: 240

BEGINNER: 20%

INTERMEDIATE: 36%

ADVANCED/EXPERT: 44%

SNOWMAKING: 70% coverage

AVG. ANNUAL SNOWFALL: 260 in.

LIFTS: 5; 2 quads, 1 double, 2 surface lifts

TERRAIN PARKS/HALFPIPES: 1 terrain park, no halfpipes

INFO: 418-632-5876; www.lemassif.com

QUEBEC

region, many people, even in tourism, just don't speak English. Then there's the complete lack of slopeside lodging. Then there's the omnipresence of competitive racing. On a given day in late February, you might be booting up in the lodge and notice two muscular lads at the next table pulling on U.S. Ski Team speed suits—the government spent millions of dollars (and moved a mountain) to create a world-class racing venue. The downhill, designed by Bernhard Russi, is among the few in the East with enough vertical to meet the FIS minimum. The resort's base elevation? A mere 119 feet above sea level.

Then there's the fact that while the top of the "mountain" enjoys snowfall equal to almost anywhere in the East—260 annual inches—snowmakers can't quite keep the bottom of the hill covered early and late season. The river's sultry, salty micro-climate pushes the frost line well up the hill to about 800 feet, where a mid-station on the new Cap Maillard high-speed quad makes itself useful long before and after the bottom of the hill is skiable.

But most of all, there's the distinct feeling of "where is everyone?" Following a 10-year march of capital improvements—lifts, trails, a handsome summit lodge, the race venue—Le Massif feels and skis as big as almost anywhere in the East. But while a place this size in southern Vermont would do 600,000 visits, Le Massif set a new record last year: 115,000.

Perhaps that's about to change. Le Massif has a new owner, one who certainly knows show biz and might be ready to nudge the resort into the minds of a broader market. Daniel Gauthier used to live in nearby Baie-Saint-Paul, a well-known artist colony. Then he started a circus and ran away with it. The Cirque du Soleil, that is. The world-renowned multi-media acrobatics troupe, of which he was president and co-owner, traces its roots to the Charlevoix region.

Today's Le Massif breaks into three distinct sections, each with a chairlift. The Baladeuse double area, on the east edge (skier's left), has a quiet, remote feel. The central section is where the action is, as well as the most direct views of the river. Here, the best of the new trail work is L'Archipel, a gladed section skier's right of the Grand Pointe Express liftline, where islands of trees lend an air of solitude. Most of the new trails are at the western edge, descending from the Cap Diamont summit and serviced by the Maillard quad and mid-station. La 42, said to be named for its angle of incline (hmm...maybe in places), used to be the only trail on Cap Diamont. It's a steep, natural-snow mogul run that requires deep cover, remains the toughest trail, almost worthy of its double-black designation.

QUEBEC

Le Massif tumbles from the edge of the Canadian Shield into the channel cut by the St. Lawrence River.

Now the race trail (La Charlevoix, which is intermittently open to the public) marks a new western boundary, descending from a 100-foot man-made peak trucked in to satisfy World Cup ski racing's vertical requirements. If there's a knock against the place, it's the sameness of pitch from trail to trail. With the notable exceptions of La 42 and the race trail, the area inclines at an angle any solid intermediate will find manageable. Experts might yearn for more steeps; beginners will be intimidated, though a new J-bar-served learning slope gives them a home. Tree-skiing is forbidden, out of respect for the environment—always a part of Le Massif's mission. You won't be the only one breaking rules if you slip into the woods, but the rewards are limited, owing to the density of the vegetation. For the most part, though, the trails are uncrowded. Doglegs left and right give them character and visual interest, and there's enough terrain to keep explorers happy for a week. –J.C.

 GETTING THERE
From Quebec City
Take Highway 138 East for 45 miles and follow signs to Le Massif. Drive Time: 1 hour

QUEBEC

Stoneham Mountain Resort

STONEHAM, QUEBEC

Remember going to the circus and watching a dozen or so clowns pile out of a Volkswagen Bug? Stoneham will surprise you in a similar way, delivering far more terrain than its modest stats suggest. Couple that with Stoneham's distinct joie de vivre—music pulsating from the base lodge, skiers keeping the beat as they dance their way to the lifts, freeriders preening and showing in the massive halfpipe and terrain parks in front of the lodge, sun-worshippers reclining in the wooden benches designed for ultimate tanning—and you have an experience that's well worth a drive across the border.

The resort anchors a horseshoe-shaped valley and comprises six connected mountains, three of which are developed for skiing. All trails end in the petite base village, which has a lodge, condos, hotel, restaurants and a few shops. Nearby sister resort Mont-Sainte-Anne may be larger, but it also is exposed to the cold, damp winds blowing off the St. Lawrence River. Rather than expose you, Stoneham embraces you, wrapping you in its mountain arms, sheltering you from the wind and letting the sun blanket you with warmth. I asked a liftmate on the high-speed quad who boasted of skiing all over Quebec why he preferred Stoneham. "This area always has the best conditions," he replied. Twice-daily grooming helps insure that.

Stoneham isn't just an easy slide. Terrain parks litter the mountain, glades vary from open and inviting to tight and challenging and the au natural trails on Mountain Four will give even haughty experts pause. The real fun of Stoneham, though, is that of discovery: joy riding in the children's glade; testing yourself on a beginner's rail; swooping down the undulating slopes in front of the base lodge; attempting to glide across Kokanee bus in the terrain park; tasting crepes and *poutine* and smoked-meat sandwiches; learning that if you don't know the French word, saying it in English with a French accent often works.

VITAL STATS

SUMMIT: 2,075 feet

VERTICAL DROP: 1,380 feet

SKIABLE ACRES: 326

BEGINNER: 20%

INTERMEDIATE: 23%

ADVANCED/EXPERT: 57%

SNOWMAKING: 86% coverage

AVG. ANNUAL SNOWFALL: 140 in.

LIFTS: 11; 4 quads, 1 double, 6 surface lifts

TERRAIN PARKS/HALFPIPES: 3 terrain parks, 1 halfpipe

INFO: 800-463-6888; www.ski-stoneham.com

Stoneham's terrain park is also lit for night skiing.

photo by Sebastien Larose

Truth is, although most folks daytrip from Quebec City, about 20 minutes south, staying in a slopeside condo is the way to go. Then you can truly experience all that this resort offers, day and night. When the sun goes down and the lights come on, Stoneham really begins to rock. Night skiing attracts a multi-generation partying crowd that seems to divide their time equally between the terrain parks, trails and the Bar of the Four Fireplaces, which has to be one of the best designed ski bars, anywhere. Especially at night, Stoneham embodies an infectious energy that few areas possess. It's lively. It's fun. And even if you don't speak a word of French, you can't help but enjoy yourself. –H.N.

GETTING THERE
From Quebec City

Take Route 175 North 15 miles and exit at Stoneham.
Drive Time: .5 hours

THE BEST OF THE REST OF QUEBEC

Eastern Townships

Most Europe-bound skiers go as much for the culture, the food and the hum of a foreign language as they do for the skiing. A trip to Quebec's Eastern Townships is like that: French country-style auberges, foreign street

QUEBEC

signs and quaint towns are as much a part of the experience as skiing the Townships' four main resorts. Of course, the Alps would tower over the Townships on a relief map. But then, the Alps aren't less than 15 miles from the Vermont border. And there's never been a better time to venture north, with the Canadian dollar hitting all-time lows against a strong U.S. dollar.

The Eastern Townships' four resorts make a rough square, each 15 to 30 miles from the next. Mont Orford and Bromont, at the two northern corners of the square, are the more modern resorts, with high-speed lifts, extensive snowmaking and up-to-date facilities. Mont Sutton, at the southwest corner of the square, evokes the ambiance of skiing's past, with its wooden base lodge and intermingling natural-snow trails. Owl's Head also has an old-fashioned feel, along with the greatest vertical drop of the four. You're likely to hear more English there than at the other three resorts combined.

With four resorts in such close proximity, it's difficult to choose just one town in which to stay. If you prefer a lively town, choose Magog. It's near Mont Orford, on the shore of 33-mile-wide Lake Memphremagog. Stroll along the brick walkways of Magog's neon-lit strip, which lasts a few blocks, and you'll pass restaurants and nightclubs. Most Township establishments accept U.S. dollars at a reasonable exchange rate, though you're usually better off buying Canadian dollars beforehand. Store clerks and resort and restaurant staff will most likely speak to you politely in their best English.

Other lodging options can be found in the picturesque town of Sutton, near Mont Sutton. All four resorts have ski-in–ski-out lodging. –B.S.

Mont Orford
MAGOG, QUEBEC

If you're staying in Magog, it's just a couple of miles to Mont Orford. The ski area has a simple layout: one centralized base area anchors a wonderful array of novice and intermediate terrain. There are three peaks. On Mont Giroux, the smaller of the three, novices will enjoy Familiale, which is long and gentle and, like many Orford Trails, wide. Two chairs access the second peak, known simply as Mont Orford, one a high-speed triple. Here you'll find pockets of expert terrain, including some triple-diamond trails (called "pistes sauvages"), which are ungroomed double-diamonds. The triple accesses Grand Coulée, a long, twisty intermediate run where skiers picnic on trailside rocks when the weather is fair.

QUEBEC

Another warm-day lunch option is the deck of the base lodge. In the spring, the resort cranks up the barbecue and hires bands. The food is reasonably priced, especially for Americans. Take it out on the deck and watch the action at the "Tube Shack," a lift-served tubing area. If you're traveling with children—or adults who behave as children—tube rides are a fun and easy diversion. For non-skiing children, Kinderski, Orford's daycare center, is a pleasant way to pass an afternoon. It's filled with giant Lego-block walls, toy wagons, smiling kids and an attentive staff. —B.S.

VITAL STATS

SUMMIT: 2,800 feet
VERTICAL DROP: 1,772 feet
SKIABLE ACRES: 170
BEGINNER: 28%
INTERMEDIATE: 37%
ADVANCED/EXPERT: 35%
SNOWMAKING: 80% coverage
AVG. ANNUAL SNOWFALL: 161 in.
LIFTS: 8; one 8-pasenger gondola, one 6-pasenger chair, 3 doubles, 3 surface lifts
TERRAIN PARKS/HALFPIPES: 1 terrain park, 1 halfpipes
INFO: 819-843-6548; www.orford.com

GETTING THERE
From Montreal

Take Highway 10 East to Exit 115 North. Follow signs to Mont Orford
Drive Time: 1 hour

From Quebec City

Take Highway 20 West to Route 55 South. Take Highway 10 West to Exit 118. Follow signs to Mont Orford
Drive Time: 2 hours

From Vermont

Take Highway 91 North. Highway 91 turns into Canadian Highway 55 at border. Take Highway 10 West to Exit 118.
Drive Time: 1.5 hours

Ski Bromont
BROMONT, QUEBEC

With lots of night skiing and a new high speed quad, Bromont offers modernity while maintaining its local charm. Attendants there help you unload your skis from your car when you arrive. On some especially cold

QUEBEC

days, they'll even offer you free hot chocolate. While you wait in line at the high-speed quad, one of the owner's two golden retrievers might approach with a stick and an unspoken request that you throw it for him. Later you might spot the same dog racing skiers down the hill.

The quad accesses the summit, where there are options for everyone. Knowlton is a moderate expert run. Twisty Montreal is slightly more challenging—and great fun. Many trails have "modulations" on the surface—spines and rolls that have been added during the past few seasons. Cowansville, an intermediate trail from the summit, has plenty of them. Many trails are groomed on one side only, so a skier who prefers corduroy can stay with a bump-bashing friend. Bromont has some *sous-bois* of its own—some marked, some not. The snowboarders, who feel at home here, are especially fond of Bedford. –B.S.

VITAL STATS

SUMMIT: 1,007 feet
VERTICAL DROP: 410 feet
SKIABLE ACRES: 161
BEGINNER: 23%
INTERMEDIATE: 21%
ADVANCED/EXPERT: 48%
SNOWMAKING: 85% coverage
AVG. ANNUAL SNOWFALL: 150 in.
LIFTS: 5; 3 quads, 1 double, 1 surface lift
TERRAIN PARKS/HALFPIPES: 1 terrain parks, 1 halfpipes
INFO: 450-534-2200; www.skibromont.com

 GETTING THERE
From Montreal

Take Highway 10 to Exit 78. Exit towards Bromont, cross the traffic light on Boulevard Bromont and turn right on Champlain to Ski Bromont.
Drive Time: 1 hour

Mont Sutton
SUTTON, QUEBEC

If you ski Mont Sutton, you'll have a very different experience from the Townships' northern resorts. "Mont Orford and Bromont are modern, like sports cars," observes one Townships local. "Sutton is like a four-by-four: wild and natural." The clientele is different, too, says the same local. "You're likely to see lace-up leather boots, old skis and snowmobiling clothes. It's that type of place where you'd expect people to carve their initials in the wooden tables in the base lodge."

Sutton's ungroomed glades give it a wild feel.

Sutton's trails fall all over each other and tumble into the trees. Many are ungroomed, natural-snow delights. It's nearly impossible to keep track of which trail you're on from one moment to the next: Start out on Sous-bois II, and you'll likely be on Traverse before you realize you did a stint on Alouette. The woods trails—known as "sous-bois" (literally, "under wood")—are usually open regardless of snow conditions. Most are fairly sparsely treed, making them accessible to intermediates.

Unlike its trails, Sutton's layout is simple. The summit, on the left as you gaze up the mountain, is the highest point on a ridge that gradually drops off as you look to the right. To the far right are the easy trails; in the middle are the intermediate runs; and to the far left the expert terrain, which comprises 38 percent of the resort. The summit, which has one intermediate trail, is worth checking out if you can, if only for its unique wooden lodge. Inside, its circular fireplace is often rimmed with drying gloves. You're likely to be surrounded by polite, French-speaking 20- to 30-year-olds, mostly men. It's a pleasant respite from the howling wind, which can be brutal at the summit when it's northerly. —B.S.

VITAL STATS

SUMMIT: 3,175 feet
VERTICAL DROP: 1,500 feet
SKIABLE ACRES: 174
BEGINNER: 17%
INTERMEDIATE: 45%
ADVANCED/EXPERT: 38%
SNOWMAKING: 60% coverage
AVG. ANNUAL SNOWFALL: 185 in.
LIFTS: 9; 3 quads, 6 doubles
TERRAIN PARKS/HALFPIPES: no terrain parks, no halfpipes
INFO: 450-538-2545; www.mt-sutton.com

QUEBEC

GETTING THERE
From Montreal

Take Highway 10 East, via Champlain Bridge to exit 68. Take 139 South to Sutton and go left onto Maple Road to Mont Sutton.

Drive Time: 1.5 hours

From Quebec City

Take Highway 20 West to Route 55. Take Route 139 South to Sutton. Turn left on Maple Road to Mont Sutton.

Drive Time: 2.5 hours

Owl's Head
MANSONVILLE, QUEBEC

If you enjoyed Sutton's retro feel, give Owl's Head a try. It is almost as old-fashioned as Sutton. In the base lodge, you'll find real skiers in old ski clothing putting on their gear as a big black dog roams around. All the pertinent services—lift tickets, rentals, etc.—are close together and easily accessible.

Experts and intermediates should head immediately to the B Chair, a quad that accesses the summit, where the view, arguably the best in the Townships, includes Lake Memphremagog. To get the most of the vertical drop, take the intermediate Lilly's Leap to Upward Trail. Much of the terrain is actually below the "base" lodge. There are plenty of wide cruisers, and some nice beginner terrain off the C and E lifts.

At Owl's Head, you'll find that everything from the trail names to the resort personnel is predominantly anglophone. That's because a ski club from West Island, the English-speaking part of Montreal, began coming here in the Sixties, and other English-speakers followed. Or perhaps it's because much of the surrounding area is also anglophone.

Or perhaps it's just that Owl's Head is the closest Township resort to the

QUEBEC

VITAL STATS

SUMMIT: 2,480 feet

VERTICAL DROP: 1,772 feet

SKIABLE ACRES: 86

BEGINNER: 34%

INTERMEDIATE: 33%

ADVANCED/EXPERT: 33%

SNOWMAKING: 90% coverage

AVG. ANNUAL SNOWFALL: 235 in.

LIFTS: 8; 4 quads, 4 doubles

TERRAIN PARKS/HALFPIPES:
no terrain parks, no halfpipes

INFO: 450-292-3342;
www.owlshead.com

border. Drive less than 15 miles, and you're back in Vermont. It's not a bad commute, considering that you just hit the slopes in a foreign land. —B.S.

GETTING THERE
From Montreal

Take Highway 10 East to Exit 106 South. Take Road 245 South to Road 243 South. After Masonville, follow signs to Owl's Head.

Drive Time: 1.5 hours

 LODGING
Auberge Hatley
North Hatley, Quebec

Among the trio of stellar inns that circle Lake Massawippi, the sleeping quarters at Auberge Hatley—a many-gabled 1902 country manse that's part of the esteemed Relais et Chateaux confederation—are the cushiest. In contrast to the spacious sitting rooms, which are warm and cozy with antiques, the 25 bedrooms are light and airy, playing off the lake views with pastels and sunny earth tones. Each has its own charm. Many boast such extras as a canopy bed, balcony, fireplace or Jacuzzi—in some cases all of the above. There also happens to be a distinguished French restaurant on the premises, provisioned by the inn's own rainwater-irrigated organic greenhouse. Info: 819-842-2451; www.relaischateaux.fr/hatley —S.M.

DINING
Manior Hovey
Lake Massawippi, Quebec

About 10 miles east of Mont Orford, Manoir Hovey—a 1900 country estate modeled after Mount Vernon—combines the best of retro-style après-ski warmth with cutting-edge cuisine. Cocktails are dispensed beside the 10,000-brick hearth in the Tap Room, which is a former carriage house bedecked with an ancient birch-bark canoe. Upstairs, in a grand lake-view salon (also fire-lit), fabulous dinners unfold in three to six courses of varying complexity. Acclaimed chef Roland Menard is an undying advocate of regional cuisine. His foodstuffs are sourced so locally that neighboring farmers merit menu bylines: M. Olivier, for instance, provides the breast of mallard duck (served with a sauce of black currants from the Île d'Orleans); M. Gagnon the rabbit that

QUEBEC

becomes a cardamom-scented *ballotin* set amid hearts of bullrushes; and Mme. Lapierre the *pleurotes* (oyster mushrooms) that cradle a fricassée of Quebec sweetbreads. Even desserts are deliciously down-to-earth, in such confections as warm zucchini cake on a marmalade of winter squash and honey-wine sabayon. It's easy to see how Manoir Hovey consistently carries off its "best of" awards—not just locally (there's keen competition among the leisure-oriented Eastern Townships), but province-, country- and even continent-wide. It's truly a national treasure. Info: 800-661-2421; www.maoirhovey.com—S.M.

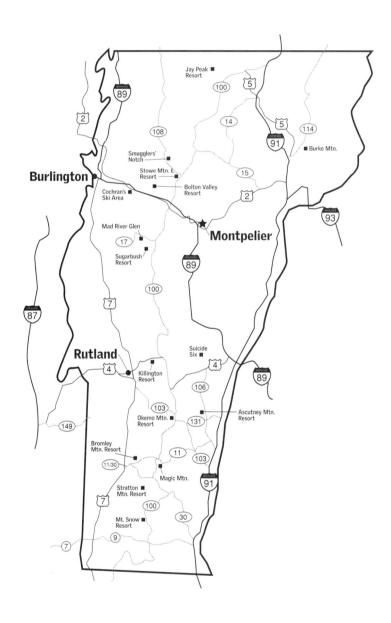

Vermont

SKI MAGAZINE'S GUIDE TO NEW ENGLAND AND QUEBEC

Killington Resort

KILLINGTON, VERMONT

No wonder Killington cracks the top ten in *SKI* Magazine every year: It's got an elementary formula. Take a big mountain (Vermont's second highest) with an unending variety of terrain (1,200 skiable acres), then make enough snow to vanquish the vagaries of New England weather and add a nightlife that won't quit. Skiers will come, bringing the energy that makes Killington unbeatable for its joie de vivre. But "the beast of the East" and its sometimes boilerplate snow isn't for everyone. "Wear your helmet," one *SKI* reader jabs. And the slopes do get busy: "I get tired of skiing on the edges of trails to find snow because of all the people," another *SKI* reader says. But as one enthused *SKI* reader stammers, "T-t-t-terrain—seven mountains' worth!" And that may be all that needs to be said about Killington. Like a Vail of the East, the Big K simply goes on and on—it's so big you could never ski it in a day, maybe not even in a week. Some readers find it overwhelming—and overcrowded. ("Weekends are crazy," a *SKI* reader complains.) But most praise the diversity of experience that such a vast resort offers, with acres of trails and glades crisscrossed by the East's largest lift network. Killington is always last in one aspect almost every year, but this is a good thing: The resort takes pride in being the last ski area to close each season, often stretching a couple of runs into the beginning of June.

VITAL STATS

SUMMIT: 4,241 feet

VERTICAL DROP: 3,050 feet

SKIABLE ACRES: 1,182

BEGINNER: 30%

INTERMEDIATE: 39%

ADVANCED/EXPERT: 31%

SNOWMAKING: 70% coverage

AVG. ANNUAL SNOWFALL: 245 in.

LIFTS: 31; 2 high-speed gondolas, 12 quads, 6 triples, 4 doubles, 7 surface lifts

TERRAIN PARKS/HALFPIPES: 2 terrain parks, 1 halfpipe

INFO: 802-422-3333; www.killington.com

SKIING IT

The beauty of size is variety. Tucked into Killington's many peaks is a ski experience for everyone, from the tamest beginner to the craziest thrill seeker. "Despite the size and glitz, it's still a skier's mountain," contends one *SKI* reader who's undoubtedly a fan of the groomed steeps found in the Canyon, or of the fabled Outer Limits, the bump trail to beat

Killington's lift network includes two high-speed, heated gondolas.

all bump trails. There's over 60 miles of groomed terrain, but for those of you who crave gnarly, head to Wild Thing and Fusion Zone, where grooming machines are not welcome.

With long cruisers like The Jug, Bittersweet and Cruise Control, and just under 40 percent of Killington's terrain designated blue square, intermediate skiers dig Killington, too. Most of the intermediate fun is packed onto Skye Peak, where you'll not only find dozens of cruisers, but also the superquick Skye Ship gondola. Killington is also a great place for intermediates to cut their teeth in the glades. Rime, East Glade and West Glade are lovely and woodsy, but tame and spread out enough to lure any level of skier into the trees. For the intermediate just ready to make the leap to expert runs, the double-fall-line Upper Double Dipper in the Canyons offers a manageable challenge.

And beginners? Killington gives them an entire peak to themselves. The Snowshed area is gentle, easily accessible and devoid of crazy skiers, which leaves the slopes to those who prefer a slower pace. But really, beginners can go almost anywhere at Killington; the area's catwalks make every peak a place slower skiers can meander down safely while taking in the sights. Then there's Juggernaut, which at 6.6 miles is said to be the longest beginner cruiser anywhere.

FAMILY MATTERS

Though Killington has earned its reputation as the ultimate party hill, lately it's been attending to families. The "beast" is looking more like

Barney these days, with fireworks displays, state-of-the-art childcare, tubing, teen programs and family-friendly accommodations.

Killington's Ram's Head facility is the resort's best attempt at marketing to families. It's home to the daycare and children's ski school, as well as all kids' rentals and other such needs. Check in is a snap, giving parents everything they need in one stop (as opposed to having to run from the ticket window to the rental shop to the ski school). Instructors are well chosen, and the program works at accommodating children with all kinds of needs. For a place long said to be kid-unfriendly, Killington has made a complete turnaround.

Nighttime can be fun for kids, too—fireworks, tubing and, if you really love your kids, a moonlight ride up the gondola for a mountaintop dinner, are all available. But after a day spent roaming seven peaks, they'll probably crash early.

GETTING THERE
From Boston
Take I-93 to I-89 North to Exit 1. Take U.S. 4 West to Killington.
Drive Time: 3 hours

From Hartford
Take I-91 to Exit 6. Take Route 103 to Route 100 North. Take U.S. 4 West to Killington.
Drive Time: 3 hours

From New York City
Take I-87 Exit 24. Take I-87 North Exit 20 (Fort Ann/ Rutland). Take Route 149 East to U.S. 4 East to Killington.
Drive Time: 5 hours

LODGING
Killington Grand Resort Hotel and Conference Center
Killington, Vermont

Sitting at the base of the Snowshed Learning Area, the $20 million Killington Grand Resort Hotel offers something that the condo-heavy resort once lacked: an upscale, full-service, centralized lodging option.

The 194,093-square-foot slopeside hotel has 200 rooms, ranging from hotel rooms to one-, two- and three-bedroom suites and penthouses fully equipped with kitchens and other amenities. For eating, it's got a full-service restaurant and an informal cafe. Valet parking, on-site childcare, concierge, bell and room service, owners' ski lockers and an exclusive owners' club round out the amenities available.

For non-skiing diversions, there's a heated 25-yard, year-round outdoor swimming pool, health club and full spa services (whirlpools, steam rooms, saunas and in-room massage). A free shuttle runs from the hotel up and down Killington's famed access road. Info: 888-64-GRAND.

Resort Condos
Killington, Vermont

Killington has long been known for its wealth of slopeside condos. From the basic and affordable like Whiffletree to the more modern and luxurious like Fall Line, there's a condo to fit every need. Condo access roads give many of the units ski-in–ski-out access. The others are serviced by a convenient shuttle system, so even if you're off the trail a bit, you'll never need to start your car. Info: 877-4-KTIMES

The Woods Spa
Sherburne, Vermont

This 105-unit resort one minute from Killington offers a wide range of massage and body treatments, plus a full-service salon. Guests get free use of spa facilities, which include an indoor pool, sauna, steam room, weight room and Jacuzzi. Body therapy is available for additional fees. During peak ski season, a three-night stay in a two-bedroom, two-bathroom suite (the smallest units sleep four) is very reasonably priced. Spa packages are available. Info: 802-422-3100

Cortina Inn and Resort
Killington, Vermont

Located just down the road from Killington, this resort offers a fusion of the rustic and sublime. The two-story stucco building rambles in a truly Vermont kind of way, with canopied terraces and wood touches. Comfortable yet trendy couches are everywhere, and the interesting local art on the walls is for sale. With 96 rooms, there's a style for everyone. Couples will love the romance of the place, but families will also be comfortable, particularly in the bunk-bed rooms. There's a skating pond and nighttime sleigh rides, along with such amenities as restaurants, room

The nightlife at Killington is as alluring as the skiing.

service, massage and even a daily bird-watching trek. Info: 802-773-3333, 800-451-6108; www.cortinainn.com

DINING
Hemingway's
Killington, Vermont

Hemingway's owner-chef Ted Fondulas says the main inspiration for his restaurant came from time spent traveling throughout Provence, France, dining in local establishments and "nosing around" in their kitchens. In 1982, he decided it was time to settle down and open his own restaurant in "a place that wasn't a city." Killington fit the bill, and Fondulas saw in an historic 1860s house (a former stagecoach stop) the potential for a dining atmosphere that could match his daring, French-inspired cuisine.

Today, Fondulas serves food reflecting his singular palate in an elegant setting that includes three old-world dining rooms (albeit ones filled with a rotating collection of abstract art). Sticking "close to the bone" with locally raised and grown products and produce, he presents seared diver scallops with corn, chives and a hint of vanilla, and rack of lamb with a zucchini, fennel and wild mushroom timbale. Homemade morel-, shiitake- and chanterelle-filled ravioli is finished with duck and truffle consommé. Pheasant, house aged and tenderized, may end up in strudel or as confit. Info. 802-422 3886   L.H.

Jackson House Inn
West Woodstock, Vermont

The Florin family of Argentina acquired this handsome Victorian landmark in 1996 and set about enhancing and expanding it. Even if you don't succeed in scoring one of its 15 luxurious rooms, you still stand a good chance—with timely reservations—of claiming one of 45 hand-fashioned cherry armchairs in the airy dining room. With its beautiful freestanding granite fireplace, the loft-like space overlooks four acres of snow-covered gardens with the requisite mountain backdrop. The atmosphere feels more expectant than formal, and as the wait staff ceremonially presents successive courses, inchoate hopes expand into joy. The menu evolves daily, in sync with the bounty of the season, but among the standards worth seeking out are the sweet lobster acorn-squash bisque with anise crème fraiche and the lyrical cider-poached salmon. City sophisticates, recognizing a spectacular find when they taste one, will want to revisit religiously. Info: 802-457-2065, 800-448-1890; www.jacksonhouse.com —S.M.

Casey's Caboose
Killington, Vermont

Casey's Caboose is the perfect setting for a family who wants to relax and still get great food. Each room is a bit different—one has Japanese tables where you sit on the floor, another is in a "tower" and looks like a caboose. You can also dine in the plow car, a 35-ton circa-1900 railroad car, or in a raised observation deck, from which an engineer once controlled and directed the plow down countless miles of track. Whichever room you choose, kids will think it's cool. And everyone can find something they like on the vast American-based menu. The ribs and wings are great, as are the nightly seafood and steak specials. And if your kids are a bit rambunctious, don't worry: So is everyone here. Info: 802-422-3795

Woodstock Inn
Woodstock, Vermont

Daniel Jackson, executive chef of Vermont's historic Woodstock Inn & Resort, is making some history of his own. Since he took over in May of 2000, the food at the Inn's famed Dining Room has evolved from traditional New England–style to what he calls "regional American."

For Jackson, it's a theme that began at the Culinary Institute of America in Hyde Park, New York. "Our instructors were concentrating on food from different regions of the country, as opposed to just French food, which had been the trend for so long," Jackson says. "That exploration made a big impression on me." Tenures at resort properties in Charleston, South Carolina, and Longboat Key, Florida, provided additional influences.

When diners open their menus in the candlelit restaurant (elegantly appointed with crisp white linens, fine table settings and soft, cream-colored décor), they find offerings such as chilled Gulf shrimp martinis, a twist on the traditional shrimp cocktail, flavored with Absolut Citron cocktail sauce and a splash of vermouth and served in a martini glass. Chilean sea bass is glazed with miso; crab cakes come with a spicy rémoulade; and fava bean cassoulet accompanies roasted rack of lamb.

That doesn't mean you won't find local products. Vermont cheese flavors the cheddar cornbread sticks. Veal tenderloin is wrapped in locally smoked bacon. Vermont beef is served carpaccio-style with black truffles and local asiago. Atlantic salmon and Maine lobster appear in varying preparations.

How does the restaurant's clientele respond to Jackson's fare? "We hear all good things from our customers," he laughs. "People come from New York, Boston, Connecticut and many of them return."

Info: www.woodstockinn.com; 800-448-7900 —L.H.

 EVENTS

Holiday in the Hills

Celebrate the kickoff to the holiday season Killington-style. Each year's festivities include the Mr. and Mrs. Claus Party, free sleigh rides, an official tree lighting and a dazzling fireworks show. Held in early December.

Budweiser All Star Aerial Show

Watch in amazement as Olympians, World Champions and National Team skiers and snowboarders launch, twist, turn and flip in the air and, more amazingly, land (most of the time, anyway). The show is complete with fireworks, music and an emcee. Held in mid January.

Sunshine Daydreams

This one is a Killington classic: Calling all Deadheads or anyone else, looking for spiritual enlightenment, Grateful Dead cover tunes, free Ben & Jerry's ice cream, tie dying, crafts, vendors and, of course, spring skiing. Held in late March.

Bear Mountain Mogul Challenge

If you want to tackle Outer Limits or just cheer on the competitors while taking in some made-for-TV crashes, you won't want to miss this weekend-long event. Mogul Challenge is packed with live music, delicious food and drinks, and tons of hip people looking for a good time. Held mid April.

INSIDER TIPS

1) Lifts without lines: The Southridge triple is slow and cold but nobody rides it. Any of the six high-speed quads are usually a good bet as well.

2) Lifts to take to follow the sun: Start at Bear Mountain and take the Bear Mountain quad, then work your way west to Skye Peak quad and Needle's Eye Express. End your day in the Canyon or on Killington Peak, where it's sunnier in the afternoon.

3) What to read to find coupons and deals: *The Mountain Times* has some discounts and is Killington's bible for what to do and where to go.

4) Snow stashes: Check out the Fusion Zones—Julio, Low Rider, Squeeze Play—for pockets of good snow. Also, since so few skiers head out there, snow sticks around the Southridge area for a while.

5) Parking secret: For the fewest cars and the most convenience, use the parking next to the Skye Ship gondola on Route 4.

6) Finest meal for the lowest fare: The vodka ziti at Peppino's is a local favorite. The Cortina Inn has an all-you-can-eat pasta night every Friday and Saturday for $10.

Stowe Mountain Resort
STOWE, VERMONT

Once the sparkling jewel in the crown of North American ski resorts, Stowe is steadily regaining the stature and luster of its glory days, though Stowe's famed "front four"—National, Lift Line, Starr and Goat—never went out of style. In-the-know skiers on the East Coast will acknowledge the quartet as the most intriguing sliding on their side of the continent. Stowe's demanding terrain entreats you to be stoic and improve your technique. Less-aggressive skiers may be less enchanted: "Challenging, watch out!" a *SKI* Magazine reader warns. And *SKI* readers do whine about value and attitude. Stowe Village, accurately described by one *SKI* reader as "picturesque and romantic," retains a postcard identity separate from the resort. Shops, pubs, eateries, lodges and charming New England architecture can entertain even a dedicated non-skier for days. (The Ben and Jerry's ice cream plant is just down the road in Waterbury. The tour features free samples.) There are many signs that Stowe has turned the

VITAL STATS

SUMMIT: 4,395 feet

VERTICAL DROP: 2,360 feet

SKIABLE ACRES: 480

BEGINNER: 16%

INTERMEDIATE: 59%

ADVANCED/EXPERT: 25%

SNOWMAKING: 73% coverage

AVG. ANNUAL SNOWFALL: 260 in.

LIFTS: 12; 1 gondola, 1 quad,
1 triple, 6 doubles, 3 surface lifts

TERRAIN PARKS/HALFPIPES:
2 terrain parks, 2 halfpipes

INFO: 800-253-4754;
www.stowe.com

corner on its under-achieving days of the early 1990s. Resort President Hank Lunde has built consensus among warring factions on a "collective vision" for the future. There is basic agreement about enhanced snowmaking, an expanded Mansfield base lodge, a "hamlet-scale settlement at the foot of Spruce Peak," even a new 18-hole golf course. The folks at Stowe promise that the architecture will "rival that of any ski resort in North America." Time will tell, but it seems that Stowe is on its way to recapturing its old title of Ski Capital of the East.—S.C.

SKIING IT

At its best, a winter weekend here is as serene and magical as one anywhere in the world—depending on the weather. And it must be said: Depending on the weather in New England can be a losing proposition. Reality is rarely as bad as perception, but it can get ugly: warm, foggy rain in January; tortuous thaw-freeze cycles in February; worst of all, a foot of powder ruined by wind or crust.

In reality, today's grooming can turn blue ice to velvet overnight. And though the climate is sometimes harsh, the rewards for enduring it are often great. Not only is there the man-made beauty of Vermont—farms and villages, churches and cemeteries—there is an uncommon natural beauty as well; one that many argue is richer and more subtle than the obvious beauty of the West. It's a quality of light; the nurturing feel of the glacier-rounded mountains; the way the mist hangs in lush river valleys on soft summer mornings; the forlorn, accidental beauty of mossy stone walls disappearing into the hardwoods. Stowe epitomizes all of this.

And if Eastern skiers are known (or at least consider themselves) to be a cut above the rest, Stowe attracts the best of the best. "I'm continually awed," says resident and ski-shop manager Piper Laidlaw. "And not just on weekdays, when you've got UVM racers training here and all the locals, but even on weekends. You're riding up the chair and some guy goes screaming by in Salomon rear-entries and some ancient Yamaha 215s, and you're like, 'Who the hell was that?'"

Some of the best skiers are never seen at all. They're deep in the hardwoods, enjoying what many say is the finest tree skiing in the East: Tres Amigos, Red Sled, River Bed, Angel Food, Mini-boos, Hell Brook, The Bruce, Teardrop, Hourglass.

That's not to say Stowe is only for the hardy or insane. For the novice skier, Stowe offers up Toll Road, arguably the most scenic, enjoyable beginner trail in the nation. Toll Road winds almost three miles, meandering through trees and out into open spaces with valley vistas to die for. Stop off at the outdoor stone chapel along the way and contemplate how lucky you are. Side trails cut here and there over the years offer more pleasant meandering.

Intermediates, too, can cruise all day long, taking on runs such as Standard and Clifftrail in the Mount Mansfield and gondola section of the resort. Average skiers will occasionally find themselves yearning to give Goat or Star a shot, but here's fair warning: At Stowe, black means black. Proceed with caution.

The lift system is worthy enough–though lacking any of those sexy new toys like high-speed six-packs. The quad works well enough, taking you bottom to top in the center of the mountain. Stowe's doubles and triple back the quad up and take you to different points of the mountain. The gondola is always an answer on colder days, but be forewarned: The lines can run long, and when winds are high the gondola closes, leaving you to face-mask it on one of the other lifts. Spruce's lifts are the slowest and oldest at the resort, but one could reason that beginner skiers need more time to rest their legs anyway.

Stowe's glades are among the best in the East.

FAMILY MATTERS

For families, Stowe's apparent weakness may be its greatest strength. The resort's two peaks, Spruce and Mount Mansfield, are separated by about a half-mile of road. Shuttles run every 10 minutes between the macho Manfield chairs and the more mellow Gondola and Spruce Peak. This can be a challenge for the parent who likes to keep visual tabs on their child, as you can quite literally be on different mountains. Technology is helping to solve this dilemma. Stowe's "beeper program" lets parents enroll their kids in ski school in the morning and pick up a beeper that allows mom or dad to be contacted anywhere on the mountain. Spruce's relative isolation is what makes it ideal for learners and young kids. Its user-friendly lifts and gentle runs—Easy Street may be the most famous— are bathed in sun all day. The base area, Little Spruce, has its own quarterpipe, base lodge, sport shop, rentals, cafeteria, lockers and one of the most complete children's centers in the country.

Stowe's renowned Sepp Ruschp Ski School is headquartered at Little Spruce. Most Stowe classes gather there before graduating to Big Spruce, the Gondola and Mansfield. The atmosphere at Spruce is laid-back. No one gets bombarded by experts charging from above.

The same holds true across Stowe proper "Comfort Zones" around the mountain are designed for families and slower skiing. Traverses are plentiful and well-marked for families who like to explore the whole mountain. And, again, Toll Road offers a perfect spot for families to take a lovely run together.

Daycare is offered for children ages six weeks and up and is licensed by the State of Vermont. The provider-to-child ratio is one-to-four, and security tags are used.

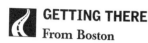 GETTING THERE

From Boston

Take I-93 North to I-89 North to Exit 10. Take Route 100 North to Stowe Village. Turn left onto Route 108 and follow to resort.

Drive Time: 3.5 hours

From New York

Take I-95 to I-91 North to I-89 North to Exit 10. Take Route 100 North to Stowe Village. Turn left onto Route 108 and follow to resort.

Drive Time: 6.5 hours

From Albany

Take I-87 North to Exit 20. Take U.S. 149 to Route 4 North. At Fair Haven take Route 22A North to Route 7 North to I-189 East to I-89 South. Take Exit 10 and Route 100 North into Stowe Village. Turn left onto Route 108 and follow to resort.

Drive Time: 3.5 hours

LODGING

Trapp Family Lodge
Stowe, Vermont

After fleeing Austria, the von Trapp family of *Sound of Music* fame settled in Stowe in 1941. They established the Trapp Music Camp and began inviting guests to stay in their lodge in 1947. After a fire, the lodge was rebuilt in 1983 and is still owned and operated by the family. There are now 116 modern rooms and 100 guest chalets. The main lodge's hand-carved balustrades, cedar-shake roofs and steeply pitched gables, along with Austrian pastry, lute lessons and family sing-alongs will make you feel as though you're in the Tyrolean Alps. The lodge serves traditional Austrian fare along with Vermont cuisine, featuring locally made products. There are common rooms with fireplaces, a fitness center with a pool and 60 km of cross-country trails. A complimentary shuttle to the ski area makes getting to the slopes easy. Horse-drawn sleigh rides, ice skating and snowshoeing make it all fun. Info: 800-826-7000; www.trappefamily.com

Stowehof Inn
Stowe, Vermont

This 45-room hotel–a 1949 memento of the Alpine fever that swept Stowe just after World War II–juts from its 30-acre hilltop like an errant Austrian ark. Recently treated to a two-million-dollar makeover by new owners Chris and Susan Grimes, the inn has retained its quirky individuality (rough maple tree trunks are incorporated into the decor of the multilevel living room), while adding new amenities, such as the Poolhof, a spa annex with indoor pool, hot tub and sauna. What hasn't changed is the front-row view of Stowe's Front Four. Info: 800-932-7136; www.stowehofinn.com

Green Mountain Inn
Stowe, Vermont

If the walls of the historic Green Mountain Inn could talk, they'd tell of fashionable guests who, in the mid 1800s, helped establish Stowe's reputation as a popular mountain resort. They would reminisce about famous visitors, such as Henry Ford, Thomas Edison, Lowell Thomas and Gerald Ford, not to mention a friendly ghost who's rumored to tap dance on the floors. As it is, they bespeak the inherent gentility of the place and foretell the hospitality that lies within.

With its red brick facade and white, 19th-century porches, Green Mountain Inn has become a local landmark. Thanks to a complete restoration (a project that took place to honor its 150th anniversary), the setting combines the tasteful, country-style elegance of the inn's early days with complete modern-day comforts and conveniences.

All totaled, the inn features 100 guests rooms and suites, the majority of which are located in the main residence. The decor includes early American-style wallpaper, stenciling and draperies, as well as reproductions of 18th-century furnishings. The adjacent Mill House (situated on the site of the historic Burt Lumber Mill) offers eight luxury suites, complete with canopy beds and Jacuzzis. The newest addition to the inn, The Mansfield House has 22 rooms and suites outfitted with everything from fireplaces to DSL internet access. Info: 802-253-7301, 800-253-7302; www.greenmountaininn.com —L.H.

DINING
Whip Bar and Grill
Stowe, Vermont

Gather for dinner at The Whip Bar & Grill in Stowe's historic Green Mountain Inn and you'll likely enjoy an experience inspired by chef Steven Truso's childhood. "I come from a large family that was always putting out big meals," the northern Vermont-born Truso explains. "The meeting place for everyone was at the table."

Named for the antique buggy whips that adorn its walls (transportation to the nearly 170-year-old inn was originally via stagecoach), The Whip attracts a convivial crowd. Locals and visitors alike warm themselves by the fire, then settle in at wooden tables topped with flowers.

In the open kitchen, which lines an entire wall of the dining room, blackboard menus announce the specials, while Truso and his staff make a show of preparing dinner. "People enjoy watching us run around in the kitchen and the flames coming up from the grill," Truso says. "Sometimes they'll come right up to the counter, with their kids on their shoulders, and watch."

The Whip has long been known as a steakhouse, but in the five years that he's been chef, Truso has upgraded the offerings. He has incorporated local ingredients into what he calls New England–style fare. Signature dishes include buttermilk flatbread (rolled thin, char-grilled, then topped with portobello mushrooms, roasted garlic and Fontina cheese); pork chops marinated in maple syrup, whole-grain mustard and apple cider; and chicken breasts stuffed with Granny Smith apples and Vermont cheddar.

Relatively new to the menu is a collection of seasonal fish dishes. In addition to popular items like Duxbury mussels steamed in white wine, garlic and butter-herb broth, the menu board will often feature herb-roasted Atlantic salmon with a zesty tomato jam.

Looking into the future, Truso foresees nothing but good times ahead. "People come up and tell us how much they enjoyed their meal. It's very satisfying." Info: 802-253-7301 —L.H.

The Chelsea Grill
Stowe, Vermont

One of Stowe's finer fine-dining options, the Chelsea Grill has garnered sparkling reviews in publications ranging from *USA Today* to the food bible *Bon Appetit*. Chef Matthew Delos, whose résumé includes a degree from the Culinary Institute of America and restaurant stints on both coasts, creates inventive gourmet lunches and dinners that match well with his extensive California-only wine list. His winter lunch menu includes a variety of gourmet pizzas, such as the wild mushroom, oregano, roasted garlic and Fontina cheese pizza, as well as smoked duck quesadillas. Dinner sees starters like the wood-fired fennel sausage soup (with spinach-and-garlic-stuffed calamari braised in a tomato caper sauce), followed by entrées including pan-roasted salmon and rosemary-braised lamb shank. It's all served in a setting that matches the splendor of the cuisine. Info: 802-253-3075

Trattoria La Festa Ristorante
Stowe, Vermont

The dining portion of La Toscana Country Inn, Trattoria La Festa offers a wide-ranging menu of pastas and traditional Italian dishes. Entrées include "Tonno alla Siciliana," a center-cut filet mignon of yellowfin tuna served with spicy white puttanesca sauce, and "Costoletta di vitello ai peperoni grigliati," grilled veal chop topped with roasted peppers and caramelized shallots, to name just two. La Trattoria's pasta dishes are also available family-style, which adds to the restaurant's air of authentic Italian gusto. Proprietors Antonio, Giancarlo and Patricia go to great lengths to assemble their selection of Italian-only wines. Annual trips to Italy assure the best vintages are selected, and the wine public has taken notice: La Trattoria has been featured in *Wine Spectator* Magazine, which called the restaurant's wine offerings "one of the most outstanding wine lists in the world." High praise, indeed. Info: 802-253-9776, 800-245-5118

The Pizza Joint
Stowe, Vermont

You can get a plain cheese pizza here, but why would you want to? With "designer pizzas" like the Kansas City BBQ (barbecue sauce, maple-smoked chicken, andouille sausage, peppers and onions), the Curaçao (Indonesian peanut sauce with chicken, broccoli and red peppers), and the South Beach (sun-dried tomato tapenade, roasted garlic, broccoli and mushrooms), pepperoni sounds pretty dull. However, if you insist, there are all the traditional toppings, plus an assortment of salads, pastas, starters and subs. Info: 802-253-4172

Stowe Village retains its picturesque New England identity separate from the resort.

Miguel's Stowe Away
Stowe, Vermont

Even if you haven't have been to Miguel's, it's quite possible you recognize this restaurant's name from its eponymous line of salsas and tortilla chips that are available at supermarkets across the country. Well, the restaurant is how it all started, and the food here is always fresh and delicious. The Super Nachos are a mountain of a meal unto themselves, and the classic Mexican dishes—like the enchiladas and chimichangas—will surely be some of the best you've ever eaten. Pricier, more elaborate fare, including several south-of-the-border variations on steak and chicken, are also available. Info: 802-253-7574, 800-245-1240

Mist Grill
Waterbury, Vermont

Who would have guessed that such a cool building—an 1807 brick grist mill—lay hidden within a stone's throw of I-89? Just some top-notch foodies who happened to be living nearby and got the notion to reverse a couple of letters and open a restaurant. If you're heading for Stowe, this stop is a must. Don't be dissuaded by the laid-back little bakery; the action is downstairs, in a granite-walled snuggery where elements of the mill have been put to creative use. The coffee—hand-roasted on-site—is reason enough to stop in. While you're at it, you might as well breakfast on hot apple pie with cheddar, lunch on pulled-duck panini or dine on chive-crusted rack of lamb. All are state-of-the-art which is not surprising, considering co-owner Steve

Schimoler, chairman of ChefExpress.net, does R&D for chefs across the U.S. The Mist's piece de resistance is a Sunday-night "family supper," where a half-dozen blackboard specials are dished out to in-the-know aficionados. Info: 802-244-2233

Black Locust Inn
Waterbury Center, Vermont

The skiing during the weekend at Stowe had been memorable, but every time I talked to a friend, the first thing I brought up was the breakfast at the Black Locust Inn. The first course, a raspberry poached pear with kiwi-strawberry sorbet, was followed by a strawberry muffin. The main course was zesty orange French toast garnished with Ben & Jerry's ice cream. The inn, an elegantly restored 1832 farmhouse with six guest rooms with private baths, is owned and operated by Len and Nancy Vignola and their daughter, Valerie.

The Vignolas, who are uniquely qualified to run an inn, act as though they are welcoming old friends into their country home. Len has a Master's degree in wine from the Waldorf Astoria Wine and Beverage Program. Après ski, he invites guests to join him by the fire to taste some vintages from his international collection. Accompanying the tasting might be Valerie's homemade bread and Vermont Common crackers with exquisite homemade artichoke-garlic dip and mushroom pâté.

The inn is 12 miles from Stowe, 20 miles from Sugarbush and Mad River Glen and close to plenty of cross-country and snowshoeing terrain (the Vignolas provide complimentary snowshoes). Not surprisingly, the inn attracts an equal number of cross-country and downhill skiers. When we visited, the downhill skiers at breakfast were debating the day's destination; taking the previous night's 10 inches of snow into consideration, they left for Mad River Glen. The more mellow cross-country skiers were lucky; they lingered over the gourmet coffee and gobbled down a few extra slices of the delicious French toast. Rates for a double room are exceptionally reasonable and include breakfast and afternoon snacks. Info: 802-244-7490, 800-366-5592 —S.M.

INSIDER TIPS
1) Lifts without lines: The Big Spruce double on Spruce Mountain offers great cruisers, some steeps and barely a line.

2) Lifts to take to follow the sun: Start at the Mansfield section and work your way north, beginning with the quad, moving to the triple, the double and then the gondola. For end-of-day sun, south-facing Spruce is your best bet.

3) What to read to find coupons and deals: *The Stowe Reporter.*

4) Snow stashes: The woods. Stowe has plenty of them so a dive off almost any trail brings a find. The woods off Big Spruce remain untouched the longest.

5) Parking secret: No one ever parks at Big Spruce. You have to take a shuttle to the Mansfield base, but it's worth it.

6) Finest meal for the lowest fare: The Whip at the Green Mountain Inn for affordable American gourmet. Mesamais, on Mountain Road close to the village, for affordable French.

Smugglers' Notch Resort
SMUGGLERS' NOTCH, VERMONT

Smugglers' has garnered top North American family resort honors from *SKI* Magazine so consistently it's nearly earned itself a Webster's entry. But beyond the first definition of well-crafted programs and friendly, furry mascots like Mogul Mouse, you'll find enough menacing terrain to make even extreme skiers like Glen Plake goofy. With three interconnected peaks— Morse Mountain, Madonna Mountain and Sterling Mountain—and a slopeside village to park your worries, Smuggs' offers something for everyone. As one *SKI* reader puts it, "Just for families? This mountain will whip any expert into shape, guaranteed." On the hill, it's classic New England cruisers, 800

VITAL STATS

SUMMIT: 3,640 feet
VERTICAL DROP: 2,610 feet
SKIABLE ACRES: 310
BEGINNER: 22%
INTERMEDIATE: 53%
ADVANCED/EXPERT: 25%
SNOWMAKING: 62% coverage
AVG. ANNUAL SNOWFALL: 284 in.
LIFTS: 8; 6 doubles, 2 surface lifts
TERRAIN PARKS/HALFPIPES:
  1 terrain park, 2 halfpipes
INFO: 800-451-8752;
  www.smuggs.com

acres of boundary-to-boundary tree skiing, and vertiginous steeps like the aptly named Freefall. When the snow's fresh, Freefall is perfect training for New Hampshire's famous Tuckerman Ravine. When it's not, you can test your knees on the rock-solid razorback moguls. Most guests choose a less masochistic alternative and return to the gentle trails of Morse Mountain to watch their kids wiggle through ski school. Singles complain that "when the lifts close, so does everything else." But parents know the action just shifts to the FunZone, an indoor Romper Room for the pre-adolescent crowd, or The Outer Limits, Smuggs' oh-so-cool, teens-only yurt. As a haven for families and a haunt for in-the-know skiers, Smugglers' has created a delicious contradiction in terms: a family resort for all ages. Top-flight service in a down-to-earth atmosphere is a Smugglers' hallmark. But beneath that friendly veneer lies a skier's steely heart. Try cozying up to a bark-chewing local for the skinny on his favorite stash, and you'll likely find him as nippy as the prevailing north wind. "The Back Bowls?" a denizen of the Smugglers' outback will say, "I've heard good things about them...they're in Vail, aren't they?"

SKIING IT

The skiing at Smugglers' Notch—rustic and challenging in some parts, lovely and open in others—may well be its best-kept secret. To start the day, head to Sterling Mountain, Smuggs' centerpiece, where you can cruise on Upper and Lower Runrunner, a winding semi-steep cruiser perfect for warming up. Next, take on Upper Pipeline for a short hit of steeps that empties out onto the more forgiving Lower Pipeline. And then, if you're up for it, try Smugglers' Alley for an advanced ride all the way down. If you think you're really good and want to show the world, hit Exhibition, an expert run under the lift.

Madonna Mountain snuggles up against Sterling Mountain and offers 40 new acres of gladed terrain to complement some of the most knee-shaking hits in the Northeast, like Freefall and the Black Hole. Attack and survive the crazy bumps on FIS or the trees on the famed Doc Dempsy trail and you've earned bragging rights just about anywhere.

Smuggs' does have one fault—its lifts. To call them slow and antiquated is being polite. But management points out the silver lining in that dark cloud: Smuggs' trails stay relatively open and uncrowded, even on the busiest of days. You may wait at the bottom, but once you're up top it seems worth it.

FAMILY MATTERS

Let's say this again: As far as family ski areas go, Smugglers' Notch is unmatched. Resort owners from around the world come here to see how it's done. It starts when you arrive. If you pre-book a package, like most Smugglers' guests do, you'll arrive at the Welcome Center to find all the necessary paperwork, from lift tickets and lessons certificates to dining discounts and directions, presented to you in a single tidy packet. And things just get easier and more convenient from there.

But it's more than just convenience. Most ski resorts focus on family by entertaining the kids separate from the adults. Smugglers' does it by creating family-bonding experiences. Some are downright corny, like family karaoke night and the Thursday night Showtime Theater skits put on by ski school, but others are warm and cuddly, like the weekly torchlight parade and fireworks display and the mini petting zoo with goats and sheep.

A recent improvement in the ski-school check-in program makes dropping kids off a snap. And at the end of the day, with kids happy from ski school, babies happy from daycare, and mom and dad happy from a day of skiing, everyone can amble around the horseshoe-shaped village, because at Smuggs', you'll only need to start your car once—when your stay is up.

Realizing that kids love swimming come summer *or* winter, Smuggs' offers a host of indoor and outdoor pools to choose from, most with nearby hot tubs for parents to lounge in while keeping a close eye on the kids. Sleeping never came so easy after all that.

The final result is wonderful: Happy kids who don't have time to whine and, therefore, relaxed and mellow parents. In the end, it's all good.

GETTING THERE
From Boston

Take I-93 North to I-89 North to Exit 10. Take Route 100 North to Route 15 West to Route 108 South. Follow to Smugglers' Notch Resort.

Drive Time: 4 hours

From New York City

Take I-95 North to I-91 North to I-89 North. Take Exit 10 and Route 100 North to Route 15 West. Take Route 108 South to Smugglers' Notch Resort.

Drive Time: 6 hours

LODGING
Smugglers' Slopeside Lodging
Smugglers' Notch, Vermont

For a stay at Smuggs', the village lodging is really the best (and almost only) bet. The 500-plus condos that line the trailsides at Smuggs' were designed for comfortable stay-in dining. Most boast kitchens as nice if not nicer than those in any suburban home. The efficiency units offer a one-room space with dining, living and sleeping room for four. One- to five-bedroom condos come with a range of offerings, from fireplaces to balconies overlooking the slopes. Many have outdoor heated pools, all have access to them. All condos also have access to laundry. Info: 800-451-8752; www.smuggs.com

Fitch Hill Inn
Hyde Park, Vermont

Located minutes from the resort, the Fitch Hill Inn offers a lovely stay for those preferring to leave the village at night. This 1797 Vermont Federal farmhouse sits on a three-and-a-half acre hilltop a quarter-mile from Highways 15 and 100. Here, peace and quiet prevail. Guests can enjoy the magnificent views of the Green Mountains from the rocking chairs on the front porch or the swing on the front lawn or the hot tub on the deck, which stays open year round. Info: 802-888-3834, 800-639-2903; www.fitchinn.com

DINING
The Top of the Notch
Smugglers' Notch, Vermont

If you're still feeling the need for adventure at dinnertime, try a dramatic and entertaining dining experience at The Top of the Notch. Ride the lift up Sterling Mountain to a candlelit hut where you'll be served a hearty meal including appetizer, entrée and dessert. Then you'll snowshoe on starlit Sterling Pond for an after-feast adventure. Reservations can be made through Smugglers' central reservations.

Snowshoe Pizza Party
Smugglers' Notch, Vermont

The Family Snowshoe Pizza Trek is for families who want to explore the backwoods and trails surrounding the village and enjoy a family-style dinner at the Morse Highlands Lodge. Reservations can be made through central reservations.

Smugglers' Notch is home to the East's only triple black diamond.

The Hearth and Candle
Smugglers' Notch, Vermont

Located in the village, this is the most elegant dining at the resort. Adults will love the quieter, more romantic setting. Standard specials such as salmon and tenderloin are offered nightly. The more gastronomically adventurous can try some of the eclectic nouveau cuisine. Info: 802-644-8090

The Mountain Grille
Smugglers' Notch, Vermont

More on the level of family fare, this restaurant is the perfect place for that night you don't feel like cooking in your condo. Kids can dig into chicken fingers and burgers; adults will be happy with the pasta and fish dishes. Info: 802-644-1244

Riga-Bello's Pizzeria
Smugglers' Notch, Vermont

The locals' favorite for pasta and pizza at affordable prices. Dine in or take it back to the condo. Classic Italian fare done well. Info: 802-644-1141

EVENTS
Heritage WinterFest

This event celebrates the area's history and features the one-and-only Primitive Biathlon. Events include a cross-country-skiing "Poker Run," a scavenger hunt, sleigh rides, a local history slide show, Heritage Museum tours, snowmobiling, snowshoe obstacle course, animal tracking on snowshoes, a pancake breakfast, fireworks, live music and dancing and a traditional Yankee pot-roast dinner. Held in late January.

Pipe Jam

Open halfpipe competition with music, prizes and demos for intermediate to expert snowboarders. Sponsored by 99.9 The Buzz and Burton Snowboards. Held mid February.

Snowshoe Walkathon

Benefits the Ronald McDonald House. Participants secure pledges to snowshoe on a specially designed course, and the event concludes with a bonfire and prizes. Fun for all levels of snowshoers. Held mid March.

INSIDER TIPS

1) Lifts without lines: First hit the Madonna II chair for a run or two before moving to Madonna I chair or the Sterling lifts.

2) Lifts to take to follow the sun: Start at Morse Mountain on the Garden Path Trail, then move to Madonna Mountain, especially Chilcoot at midday. Afternoon means Sterling Mountain, particularly Black Snake, which gets great sun late.

3) What to read to find coupons and deals: The best coupons are at www.smuggs.com. Also, each destination guest receives a coupon book for local dining upon check-in. Plus, *The Stowe Reporter*.

4) Snow stashes: The glades rule, as do the 740 acres of woods between the marked trails (all open for skiing).

5) Parking secret: There is no secret. Park your car when you arrive; don't start it again until you leave.

6) Finest meal for the lowest fare. Riga Mello's Italian Eatery at the base area. Locals adore it.

Sugarbush Resort

WARREN, VERMONT

Sugarbush offers big-mountain terrain spread over what used to be two separate ski areas; inspiring views of the Green Mountains; and an uncommonly beautiful farming-turned-resort community unspoiled by its success. Sugarbush's two mountains—Mount Ellen and Lincoln Peak, or North and South, respectively, to the faithful—are linked via the scenic Slidebrook Express lift, which travels horizontally between the two. Either area could stand on its own. Together, they seem endless. A few *SKI* Magazine readers find Sugarbush expensive. Many can hardly find it at all, hidden as it is in the heart of northern Vermont. "Middle of nowhere," says one *SKI* reader. Off-hill, the Mad River Valley offers just enough in the way of dining, après ski (once you know where to look) and other diversions to keep the faithful happy while still keeping it real. "Laid back; no hype," says a *SKI* reader. Sugarbush has bucked the consolidation trend, going indie after a half-dozen years under American Skiing Company's corporate logo. Like a midlife rocker

VITAL STATS

SUMMIT: 4,135 feet

VERTICAL DROP: 2,650 feet

SKIABLE ACRES: 468

BEGINNER: 18%

INTERMEDIATE: 39%

ADVANCED/EXPERT: 43%

SNOWMAKING: 67% coverage

AVG. ANNUAL SNOWFALL: 260 in.

LIFTS: 18; 7 quads, 3 triples, 4 doubles, 4 surface lifts

TERRAIN PARKS/HALFPIPES: 5 terrain parks, 2 halfpipes

INFO: 800-53-SUGAR; www.sugarbush.com

suddenly free of a major-label contract, Sugarbush has shown new vigor. "Much better without ASC," swears one fan. The new management proved its mettle by replacing the antiquated Castlerock lift without increasing uphill capacity or fiddling with the rhythm of the terrain that the life serves, a handful of challenging, twisting trails untouched since their conception in the 1960s and the closest thing to church for many a Mad River Valley expert. The new team also renovated wisely at Sugarbush North—Mt. Ellen, that is—by restoring high-speed-quad service to the base of the summit chair. Returning a lift back to its logical location not only cuts the commute; it also allows the resort to offer the high-altitude early- and late-season skiing for which it was long famous. True, the 'Bush is still a long haul for southern New England skiers, but with Sugarbush's superb terrain offerings now getting the right strokes,

Sugarbush has 115 trails descending from three of the Glen Mountain's highest peaks.

American Skiing Company resorts in southern Vermont might someday regret the divorce.

SKIING IT

If you've never been to Sugarbush, the east flank of Mount Abraham presents an imposing face as you pull into the huge dirt parking lot at its base. If your gut instinct when you arrive at any ski area for the first time is to get to the summit as soon as possible, at Sugarbush you should follow your gut. Back in the day, a gondola climbed the west wall of the valley in a single shot before its colorful but cramped cars were retired in the '70s. Now you need to take two lifts: the Valley House chair, then, after a short warm-up run, Heaven's Gate chair. The latter deposits you atop the world, on 3,975-foot Lincoln Peak. You can gaze westward over the spine of the Green Mountains to Lake Champlain shimmering in the distance—a long silver sheet backed by the Adirondacks of New York— or eastward to the White Mountains of New Hampshire. To the north is another Vermont landmark, Camel's Hump—misshapen from this angle— with Mount Mansfield just beyond. Once you've got your bearings, cycle for a couple of runs on some of the resort's toughest terrain—Paradise and Organ Grinder—or mellow out on the intermediate S turns of Jester and Downspout. Depending on the weather, it might be time to retreat to a more sensible altitude. On a cold day, there's no better place to ski at Sugarbush than the sunny slopes of North Lynx Peak, on the north edge of the area. In between North Lynx and Heaven's Gate, however, is the

'Bush's signature terrain: the hallowed trails of Castlerock.

Castlerock remains today as it's always been. The lift ride is 11 minutes, servicing 2,237 vertical feet of classic New England terrain that's only open when there's ample snow. With the chair acting as capacity regulator, it's not uncommon to turn a corner on Rumble or Middle Earth or Castlerock Run and find yourself alone amid the quiet of the forest. But don't be mesmerized: The terrain, never groomed, demands full attention. After two runs on Rumble—probably the resort's toughest trail—your stomach will be rumbling, too. Lucky for you, Sugarbush has one of the best slopeside dining experiences anywhere in North America. Find your way to Chez Henri (just across the covered walking bridge north of the base area), where proprietor Henri Borel still presides over a classic French bistro experience.

After lunch, there won't be time or inclination to make the Slide Brook Express connection to Mount Ellen (Sugarbush North). It's better to explore what's left of South. Board the Super Bravo quad again and head to the southern edge of the area. On the way up, you can decide whether you're up for Stein's Run (Stein Eriksen briefly headed the ski school here before moving to Deer Valley, Utah). Go left off the top of Super Bravo and it's a long, easy traverse to the top of three challenging black diamonds: Stein's, The Mall and Twist. Keep going, and you'll find easier terrain on Spring Fling and Snowball, which form the southern boundary of the resort. There's rarely a line on the Valley House chair, a fixed-grip double that accesses the southern trails. And on busy weekends, intermediates can cycle on the Spring Fling triple, all the way at the southern edge of the area. There's easily enough terrain here to keep you occupied till last chair, when you can pack up the skis and set out to explore the Valley in earnest. —J.C.

FAMILY MATTERS

Unlike most resorts in the Northeast, and the nation for that matter, Sugarbush isn't spending a lot of time dubbing itself as the be-all, end-all family destination. But that's not to say they don't offer what a family needs. The ski school is solid in a traditional kind of way, with programs designed to take kids of the same ability and the same ages out on the mountain together.

Daycare takes kids from six weeks old and up. One issue is that while the daycare is located conveniently in the Sugarbush Village, once a parent gets out on the mountain, it can be a bit of a trek to get back and check in. The good news is that your child is in highly capable, state-licensed hands.

For kids who really love being on snow, check out Sugarbush's week-long freestyle skiing and riding camps. The programs can raise any kid's ski level and will keep even the most disinterested teen skier engaged and satisfied.

For family fun after skiing, the Valley itself offers ice skating, snowmobiling, snowshoeing, sleigh riding and even maple sugaring. Last but most assuredly not least, you can't make a visit here with kids without the obligatory ride up to Waterbury (about 15 minutes) for the Ben and Jerry's factory tour.

GETTING THERE
From Boston

Take I-93 North to I-89 North. Take Exit 9 (Middlesex) to Route 100B to Route 100 South. Follow to Sugarbush.

Drive Time: 3.5 hours

From New York City

Take I-95 to I-91 North to I-89 North. Take Exit 9 (Middlesex) to Route 100B to Route 100 South. Follow to Sugarbush.

Drive Time: 5.5 hours

LODGING

Sugarbush offers plenty of slopeside or walk-to-the-slopes lodging, mostly in the form of condos, though there are some hotels. For a general booking number, use 800-53-SUGAR or log on to www.sugarbush.com. Some locations to consider include:

Sugarbush Resort Condominiums
Warren, Vermont

The resort has ski-in–ski-out condos and lavish three-bedroom town-houses, and a selection of two-, three-, and four-bedroom villas. There is a wide range of pricing options.

Sugarbush Inn
Warren, Vermont

The Sugarbush Inn is a traditional country inn with single and double bedrooms, two restaurants, an outdoor hot tub and open lounging spaces with fireplaces.

Castlerock Peak features challenging bumps and ungroomed glades.

The Pitcher Inn
Warren, Vermont

The handsome, substantial white clapboard building fronts directly on Main Street and looks like a classic, but inside, the decor is hardly traditional. There are eight rooms and two suites, in which owners Margaret and Winthrop Smith encouraged multiple designers to follow their imaginations. Each room is a singular, luxurious creation. The Duck Room resembles a reedy hunting blind; the Lodge Room evokes Masonic mysticism; the Mountain Room will make 10th Mountain Division vets nostalgic. Info: 888-867-4824; www.pitcherinn.com

1824 House
Waitsfield, Vermont

This gabled farmhouse is a black-shuttered beauty in the classic "big house, little house, back house, barn" configuration. The eight rooms, each named for a Vermont county, range in size and price, but all feature sumptuous feather beds. The knockout is the spacious, pale-green Caledonia Room, a quick sprint—through French doors—from the outdoor hot tub. Also close at hand is a skating pond, lit up at night, and 22 acres open for snowshoeing, cross-country skiing and sledding. The resident Labs, a mother-daughter duo in yellow and black, might like to keep you company. In spring, you can take in the sugaring operation at the farm stand next door. Info: 802-496-7555, 800-426-3986; www.1824house.com

178

VERMONT

DINING
The Pitcher Inn
Warren, Vermont

Recreated in 1997, the Pitcher Inn was once and is again the über fine dining spot in the Sugarbush vicinity. Chef Tom Bivins goes gourmet without going overboard on fat and cholesterol, and the wine list does his art justice. Intimate dinners can be arranged in the private wine cellar. Afternoon tea and pastries and after-dinner cordials are served in the parlor on the main floor. All baked goods are prepared daily on the premises. The menus are regionally inspired and then infused with cross-cultural influences. Simple rustic ingredients are used with a strong tendency toward game for main courses. Info: 888-867-4824; www.pitcherinn.com

John Egan's Big World Grill and Pub
Waitsfield, Vermont

For family fun or relaxed hanging out, John Egan's Big World is a can't miss. With a wide variety of microbrews including their own Egan's Ale, the pub is a great place to have a drink or dinner. The menu offers a taste of every corner of the world, from Hungarian goulash to Mediterranean eggplant to a more locally inspired maple crème brûlée. They do the staples well, too, from burgers to nachos and everything in between. The real fun, though, comes in the setting. Under Plexiglas bar tops is an assortment of ski memorabilia that any snow-slider will find interesting. Info: 802-496-3033

The Spotted Cow
Waitsfield, Vermont

The Spotted Cow is a nifty little eatery paneled in red birch with cherry molding. Chef Eric Bauer, whose résumé includes Chez Henri, a Mad River Valley institution, brings his skills to bear on an elegant dinner menu, in which herb-and-garlic-crusted rack of lamb, for instance, comes napped in a Riesling black truffle sauce (the most expensive entrée option). Several dishes reflect owner Jay Young's Bermuda background, including the turbo-charged fish chowder spiked with cherry peppers and black rum, a family recipe dating to the 18th century. Also served at lunch, this high-octane bouillabaisse could fuel a hard-charging afternoon. Info: 802-496-5151

The Den
Waitsfield, Vermont

The Den has been the choice for fast, affordable, basic but delicious food going on 50 years now. Locals know to stop here for the burgers, salad bar and po'boy sandwiches. The setting is casual enough that kids blend right in, and you don't have to change out of your ski clothes. Info: 802-496-8880

 EVENTS

The Turkey Tumble Mogul Competition

This is said to be the region's first big mogul event of the season. Held on the Sunday after Thanksgiving, the event draws all levels of competitor, from wannabes to world class. Held in late November.

The Castlerock Extreme Challenge

One of the most talked about mogul competitions in the nation. Big names show up and hit the bumps hard. Held in late February.

Sugarbush Pond Skimming Competition

Taking place the first weekend of April each year, this season-end tradition is so fabled that Warren Miller has shot it for one of his films. A reggae fest and cookout round out the fun.

INSIDER TIPS

1) Lifts without lines: The new Green Mountain Express on Mount Ellen is less used than other lifts yet just as accessible to terrain.

2) Lifts to take to follow the sun: The secret at Sugarbush is the North Lynx triple, where the sun shines all day long. It serves both gladed and groomed trails.

3) What to read to find coupons and deals: *The Valley Reporter* or the *Vermont Journal.*

4) Snow stashes: Paradise and Lower Paradise off the Heaven's Gate triple typically hold snow, but better is the Slidebrook Wilderness Area, where guided access can score you 3,000 acres of usually untouched powder.

5) Parking secret: Mount Ellen in general tends to fill up later on busier days. Also, the small upper lot next to Chez Henri at Mount Lincoln tends to be ignored by people rushing into the big lower lots.

6) Finest meal for the lowest fare: "Johnny's Pasta" at John Egan's Big World Pub And Grill. A huge plate of fresh Gulf shrimp with pancetta bacon, bowtie pasta and peas, served in a delicate herbal broth. Comes with a big salad and unlimited baskets of fresh-baked bread.

Stratton Mountain Resort

STRATTON, VERMONT

Stratton is the kind of mountain fussy skiers love to hate. *SKI* Magazine readers complain about the "uneven weather" and the "need for more expert terrain," and they whine that it's "way too pricey." Consider theirs the whines of envy. Stratton caters to a tony crowd that would rather be pampered than challenged, one that prefers buffed slopes to mega-moguls. That's not to say there isn't challenging terrain here; the pitch is good, and the glades will satisfy expert skiers for at least a short visit. Still, most of the black diamonds are negotiable by confident intermediates.

VITAL STATS

SUMMIT: 2,350 feet

VERTICAL DROP: 2,003 feet

SKIABLE ACRES: 583

BEGINNER: 42%

INTERMEDIATE: 31%

ADVANCED/EXPERT: 27%

SNOWMAKING: 97% coverage

AVG. ANNUAL SNOWFALL: 142 in.

LIFTS: 16; 1 twelve-person gondola, 4 six-person chairs, 4 quads, 1 triple

TERRAIN PARKS/HALFPIPES: 6 terrain parks, 2 halfpipes

INFO: 800-787-2886; www.stratton.com

Loyal Strattonites see this ego-boosting terrain as a plus. Indeed, "well-groomed cruisers" are the resort's calling card. Stratton is especially popular with families, who praise the manicured slopes and "excellent snowmaking," as well as the family-oriented programs. Although it boasts a 2,003-foot vertical drop, making it "almost a big mountain" in the eyes of one *SKI* reader, the resort's biggest asset is its southern Vermont location. It's "easy to get to from Massachusetts, New York, New Jersey and Connecticut." The downside of this accessibility is that "it gets crowded on weekends," as one *SKI* reader gripes. But with those crowds translate into long lift lines. Since acquiring Stratton in 1994, parent company Intrawest has invested heavily in high-capacity lifts so that "even during the busiest times, you can get a lot of runs in," one *SKI* reader notes. The base village, which includes a good selection of shops and restaurants, has also received a much-needed face-lift. This village, combined with the shopping of nearby Manchester, means even non-skiers have plenty to do. "Vail East" says one *SKI* reader. A "very under-rated resort that gets better every year," says another. –H.N.

SKIING IT

Stratton is a straightforward mountain that's pretty easy to figure out. However, it can get crowded, and this is where a good game plan can help. If you're an intermediate skier or better, start your day by taking the American Express six-pack from the base directly to the URSA six-pack all the way up to the summit. Up top, you'll notice everyone heading left to the "bear runs." Ignore them and instead hang right and get in a few fast and furious cruisers on North American and Standard, both steep, double fall-line trails that few skiers hit first thing. Once you've made your mark there, head back up and take on those bear trails: Challenge your bump know-how on Grizzly, cruise a lovely blue on Black Bear, or push the speed limit on Polar Bear.

When your legs are screaming for a rest, head over to the Snowbowl lift, one of the slower chairs on the mountain. Its long ride time will give you a breather, and its Liftline run is challenging enough to take on a few times. On the other side of the mountain, the Sunbowl area offers fantastic begin-ner and intermediate terrain. For glades, start out at Emerald Forest just off the meandering Hemlock run. Emerald Forest's trees are dense enough to make you think but open enough to make you comfortable. Like it? Try Dancing Bear glade next for a bigger challenge.

If you prefer slower speeds, beginners love the lower Tamarack area with its combination of wide-open spaces and deep woods. Speed demons seldom go there, which leaves it serene for lower-level skiers.

FAMILY MATTERS

Stratton's ski instructors—an amazing 60 percent of them on the job at the ski area for more than 15 years—set aside large blocks of their time specifically for families. The regulars find their favorites and hold onto them, but visitors will fare well, too. And the resort's Little Cub and Cubs instruction programs address the skiing and boarding needs of children of every age.

Located in southern Vermont, Stratton Mountain is easy to get to from Massachusetts, New York, New Jersey and Connecticut.

Stratton's childcare program is a fully licensed facility for kids from six weeks to five years old and is open from 8 A.M. until 5 P.M. In Ski and Play, children three years old and up are based out of the childcare area but take part in an introductory program that promotes the fun and basics of skiing. The one-hour lesson is just enough for little ones, and skis and boots for the kids are right on the premises, meaning one less stop for parents in the morning.

Once children are ages four to six, they can join Little Cubs, a half-day or full-day program that gets kids out on the slopes more, but still gives them the breaks they need. Big Cubs (ages seven to 12) keeps them on the snow longer and takes on more advanced trails. For beginners from seven to 12, the Junior Newcomers program allows older kids to learn without having to be stuck with little kids (a great idea that many ski areas have yet to think of).

For family lodging, the choices are endless. Plenty of condos are available, and the new Long Trail Lodge gives families a condo feel (separate bedrooms and kitchens) with hotel treatment (concierge, pools and other amenities).

 **GETTING THERE**
From Boston
Take Route 2 West to I-91 North. Take Exit 2 to Route 30 North to Stratton Mountain Road.
Drive Time: 2.5 hours

From New York City

Take I-87 North to Exit 23. Take I-787 to Route 7 East. Route 7 becomes Route 9. Take Route 9 East to Route 7 North. Take Exit 4 and turn right onto Route 11/30. Take Route 30 South to Stratton Mountain Road.

Drive Time: 4 hours

LODGING

Along the mountain access road you'll see numerous homes, condos and hotels. Many are for rent, and most are easily booked through Stratton Central Reservations at 800-787-2886. All guests at Stratton-operated accommodations are given free access to the Stratton Sports Center, which has an indoor pool and hot tub, racquetball, tennis and a fitness center. Some choice lodgings include:

Long Trail House
Stratton, Vermont

Stratton's newest lodging facility will soon be the anchor for a new village at Stratton. From efficiencies to four-bedroom condos, all the rooms in the Long Trail are steps from the village and trails and are serviced by a concierge desk. The Long Trail House has its own heated swimming pool, hot tubs, sauna and heated private underground parking. Info: 800-974-1104

Stratton Condominiums
Stratton, Vermont

Condos dot the mountainside and typically have from one to four bedrooms, washers and dryers, fireplaces, cable TVs and more. Most are steps from the lifts. Book through central reservations.

Liftline Lodge
Stratton, Vermont

This traditional, 77-room European-style lodge is close to Stratton's ski lifts, and village shops, restaurants, and attractions. With friendly service and convenient parking, it is considered the affordable alternative on the mountain.

DINING

On and off mountain, Stratton has great variety of dining options. One on-mountain warning: the village pretty much shuts down after 6 P.M. While some restaurants do stay open, check ahead of time so you're not surprised when they're scooting you out the door. While the base lodges do offer typical fare, there's a lot more to choose from, including:

Mulberry Street
Stratton, Vermont

Located right at the entrance of the village, Mulberry Street offers a setting relaxed enough to bring the kids in for pizza, but doles up Italian main courses impressive enough to qualify as fine dining. Try the hearty veal marsala, and don't miss the martinis—Mulberry is known for them. Info: 802-297-3065

Mulligan's
Stratton, Vermont

The diverse but basically American menu has everything from great burgers to ribs, steaks, and seafood. The relaxed atmosphere is good for families or singles who just want to chill out. Info: 802-297-9293

The Blue Moon Cafe
Stratton, Vermont

Located in the center of the village, The Blue Moon's signature item is the crepe. For breakfast or lunch, they offer unique, delicious fillings. There's also a pastry selection, coffee bar and, upstairs, an après-ski piano bar that's straight out of a James Bond flick. Info: 802-297-2093

Cafe on the Corner
Stratton, Vermont

Located inside the Lift Line Lodge, this eatery offers the heartiest and most affordable breakfasts on the mountain. For a fill-me-up that will take you way past lunchtime, check out the eggs benedict, French toast, or hash browns. Info: 802-297-0141

Partridge in a Pantry
Stratton, Vermont

This is a gourmet shop and deli with breakfast sandwiches, huge gour-

Stratton's six terrain parks cover more than 45 acres.

met lunch sandwiches and creative wraps. Eat in or (as most people choose) take out. Good wine selection as well. Info: 802-297-9850

Cider's
Stratton, Vermont

Cider's serves up hearty homestyle cooking for breakfast and lunch. Their signature pancakes with hot Vermont maple syrup are much talked about, as are the lunch specials which include homemade meatloaf, southern fried chicken, turkey dinner with all the fixings and hearty soups and chowders. The food tastes like your Grandma from the South whipped it all up. Plus, Cider's has a ski-to-the-door location.

The Colonnade
Manchester Center, Vermont

For a more upscale experience, the dining room of the fabled Equinox Hotel offers an opulent setting–historic artwork, velvet curtains, fine china–with food that stands up to the atmosphere. Try such staples as the maple-mustard-glazed lamb chops on roasted shallot wild rice, or apple-roasted pheasant with wild rice and fresh berries. Info: 802-362-4700, 800-362-4747

EVENTS
Stratton Mountain Boys

When Stratton was a new kid on the block, most if not all of the ski instructors were from Austria and doubled as musicians. They'd perform daily at the base, singing Austrian folk melodies. Today, they only get together once a year, usually some time in January. It shouldn't be missed, so keep your eye on www.stratton.com for dates.

U.S. Open Snowboard Championships

Drawing the best in the world, this annual event belongs at Stratton because Stratton is, quite literally, where snowboarding was born. Held the third week of March, the Open draws the top men and women in the world and, because it is a true open-field qualifier event, always holds a few surprises.

Spring Fling Pond Skimming

Held in early April each year, skiers throw themselves down the mountain full speed in an effort to hydroplane across the pond at the bottom. A ski-area standard that never fails to amuse.

INSIDER TIPS

1) Lifts without lines: Perhaps because it's an older quad, the Snow Bowl lift is totally underused even though it serves great terrain.

2) Lifts to take to follow the sun: Start at Sun Bowl, move to Ursa Express, and finally on to Snow Bowl (the afternoon sun hits the Meadows, an easy crusier perfect for wrapping up the day).

3) What to read to find coupons and deals: Check www.stratton.com for last minute deals. Once you're in town pick up the *Manchester Journal* (particularly for dining deals).

4) Snow stashes: You'll always find snow in Kidderbrook Ravine.

5) Parking secret: Head straight to the Sun Bowl parking lot.

6) Finest meal for the lowest fare: Try Mulligan's midweek specials like a lobster bake on Mondays and Tuesdays, or the Steak and Brew deals downstairs in the Green Door Pub.

Jay Peak Resort

JAY, VERMONT

In Vermont, the word on Jay Peak passes through lift lines like a game of telephone. "Did you hear what they got at Jay?" someone asks. "Yeah," a nearby voice replies. "The radio said 12 to 14 inches and still dumping." By day's end, it's 18 to 22 with more on the way. "Yeah, right," some cynic inevitably sneers. "Who's reading the stake, Ray Charles?" But those familiar with the "Jay Cloud" just shake their heads and grin, knowing that every pessimist today is one less person skiing the powder lines tomorrow.

"When I first started working as a meteorologist," says Steve Maleski, Vermont Public Radio's "Eye on the Sky" weather guy, "people used to talk about a 'Jay Inch.'" What else could explain such wildly inflated snowfall totals? "Well, one year we compared the melted-precip data with the reported snowfall, and it squared. They're just very favorably located." The area's annual snowfall averages 351 inches and topped the 400 mark four times since 1994.

Like a lone sentinel at the top of Vermont, Jay gets hammered from three directions: southwesterlies coming up the Champlain Valley, Alberta Clippers sailing down off the Canadian Shield and cycling Nor'easters that pick up moisture from the mouth of the St. Lawrence. Throw in the multiplier of being the highest mountain in the neighborhood—a phenomenon known to meteorologists as the "orographic effect" and to locals simply as the "Jay Cloud"—and you've got snowstorms that home in on the area like ski bums to happy hour.

VITAL STATS

SUMMIT: 3,968 feet

VERTICAL DROP: 2,153 feet

SKIABLE ACRES: 385

BEGINNER: 20%

INTERMEDIATE: 40%

ADVANCED/EXPERT: 40%

SNOWMAKING: 80% coverage

AVG. ANNUAL SNOWFALL: 351 in.

LIFTS: 8; 1 sixty-passenger tram, 3 quads, 1 triple, 1 double, 2 surface lifts

TERRAIN PARKS/HALFPIPES: 1 terrain park, 1 halfpipe

INFO: 800-451-4449; www.jaypeakresort.com

Jay Peak was founded in 1956 by the local Kiwanis to promote business in this remote corner of Vermont's Northeast Kingdom. Today, it is a tribute to skiing the way it used to be, and yet it is squarely on the vanguard of the modern tree-skiing movement. Jay offers the most—and arguably best—glades this side of Steamboat. A dozen years of dogged clearing and fastidious maintenance have created a well-marked network of 24 glades

100

Jay Peak is known for its untamed glades.

and put more than 100 acres of terrain in play.

Though often compared to Jackson Hole, both for epic storms and signature tram cars, Jay Peak more closely resembles the Matterhorn. From a distance, the summit—though a comparatively modest 3,968 feet—juts skyward like the stony backdrop of a Bond flick. Up close, the 36-degree pitches and 20-foot drops of Jay's inbounds Face Chutes do recall the Jackson analogy and provide respectable training for skiers who aspire to big Western mountains.

SKIING IT

Here's what it says on the Jay Peak trail map: "Woods are not open, closed or marked." It's right there in black and white. But if for some reason you're not entirely clear on what that means, ask a Jay regular on a midweek powder day. He'll look at you funny as your steamy tram car bumps past Tower 2 and begins its final climb to the summit, then pull down his snow-crusted neck gaiter and reply: "It means ski wherever the hell you want, man. But it's your ass. Don't expect anyone to come save it if you screw up."

That is what it should say on the trail map at Jay Peak, where managers have been looking the other way since...well, long before other Eastern resorts warmed to the idea of letting customers ski where they want to. Families and casual skiers can find an abundance of easy groomers at Jay. And, yes, there are steep corduroy cruisers off the Stateside area's Jet triple chair. But Jay is mostly about untamed expert terrain, a place where a day is most productively spent off trail, searching out pockets of untracked snow on thickly forested inclines you'd swear weren't skiable if you weren't looking at someone else's tracks. No line is too narrow, nor any landing too tight for Jay locals. And if you can't live with a few sapling wounds to the face and the occasional rip in your Gore-Tex, Bretton Woods, New Hampshire, is just 90 minutes away.

If there's a knock against Jay Peak—other than its remote location and arctic climate—it's that the lifts are inadequate. But the addition of the Green Mountain Flyer—a high-speed quad dubbed the "G.M. Freezer" by local wags—has gone a long way to increase Jay's uphill capacity and improve access to the best intermediate terrain, including Ullr's and the Northway. And tram upgrades have shortened lift lines even further. Though the new tram cars are no longer Jackson Hole red, they are a couple minutes faster and fitted with no-fog windows that give passengers a bird's-eye view of the terrain.

FAMILY MATTERS

Happily, Jay isn't all wild child. In fact, the most aggressive skiing at Jay can sometimes be the race to score the chocolate-chip cookies dispensed by Moose, the lift-op at the bottom of the Queen's Highway T-bar, a lift that serves mellow, learner-friendly terrain.

Perhaps in an attempt to take the edge off its hardcore reputation, Jay lets you know that kids are welcome before you even get there: The special "snow monsters" section on the resort's website allows kids to get to know Jay in a playful way. And it's true: The steeps and woods needn't scare families off. An extensive ski-school program for all ages, a daycare for non-skiers and one-on-one babysitting for infants ensures that mom and dad can get all the freshies they want while the kids are attended to. But that's not to say you can't ski together, either. The resort's got lots of wide-open groomers. And even if you split up for a couple of runs or an entire afternoon, day's end brings everyone back together in a village that makes it easy to meet up and hang out as a family.

Jay is in the process of breaking through to four-season-resort status with a golf- and ski-based expansion. And Jay Peak Village—an "environmentally integrated" slopeside development with indoor swimming and other family-friendly amenities—will eventually add 1,200 new units, bumping Jay's meager bed base from 900 to as many as 5,000.

GETTING THERE
From Boston

Take I-93 North to I-91 North. Take Exit 26 (Orleans) to Route 5 North to Route 14 North. Take Route 100 South to Route 101 North. Turn left onto Route 242 to Jay Peak.

Drive Time: 3.5 hours

From New York City

Take I-95 North to I-91 North to Exit 26 (Orleans). Take Route 5 North to Route 14 North. Take Route 100 South to Route 101 North. Turn left onto Route 242 to Jay Peak.

Drive Time: 6.5 hours

LODGING
Village Townhouses and Condominiums
Jay, Vermont

These units, the upper crust of the slopeside offerings, define luxury at Jay Peak. There's ski-in–ski-out access, a chairlift just for the building, and units with 1,600-square feet of space. All have a full kitchen, dining and living room, gas fireplace, washer and dryer and TV/VCR. Some units have private steam baths and saunas. Units sleep up to eight guests. Info: 800-451-4449

Slopeside Condos
Jay, Vermont

Nestled into the lower mountainside in the village, these two-bedroom condos are ski-in–ski-out with full kitchens, washers and dryers, large living rooms with fireplaces and private balconies overlooking the slopes. Good for groups. Info: 800-451-4449

Hotel Jay
Jay, Vermont

This more affordable option for people who prefer a hotel atmosphere is located in the heart of the resort, just 90 feet from the tram. Each room has a queen-sized bed, private bath, cable and a private balcony. The hotel itself has a dining room, lounge, game room, family room, sauna, Jacuzzi and private ski lockers. Info. 800 451 4449

Jay Peak's annual snowfall can top 400 inches.

Stoney Path Condos
Jay, Vermont

These condos are another affordable option for skiers who don't mind a short walk to the slopes. They feature one- and two-bedroom units with up to two baths. All units have a full kitchen and a fireplace.

Bay View Lodge & Motel
Newport, Vermont

The Bay View has 17 comfortable motel-style rooms with cable TV, phone, private bath and a balcony with a view of a lake and mountains. Guests have access to a Jacuzzi, game room and sitting room with cast-iron fireplace. Packages combining lift tickets, lodging, breakfast, dinner and shuttle service to and from the ski area are available. Info: 802-334-6543; www.bayviewlodgeandmotel.com

The Black Lantern Inn
Montgomery Village, Vermont

This restored 1803 country inn, which is listed in the National Historic Register, features 10 rooms with private baths and six suites with fireplaces and whirlpool tubs. It offers fine dining in a candle-lit dining room and an outdoor hottub. Info: 802-326-4507, 800-255-8661; www.blacklantern.com

English Rose Inn
Montgomery Center, Vermont

Three and a half miles from Jay Peak, this 1850s farmhouse has 14 guest rooms decorated in a Victorian style, a fireplace room, a library and several sitting rooms. English/American breakfasts and traditional afternoon tea with fresh-baked delicacies add to the charm. Fine dining is available. Info: 802-326-3232; www.theenglishroseinn.com

DINING
The Belfry Restaurant
Montgomery Center, Vermont

Fresh fish, blackened steak, Wednesday Italian Night, homemade desserts and friendly service. That's a good combination. Info: 802-326-4400

Hidden Country Restaurant
Lowell, Vermont

Located 10 miles from Jay Peak in a rural setting with wonderful views. House specialties include prime rib, roasted whole Vermont turkey, lamb, pork and various seafood dishes. Info: 802-744-6149

JR's Cafe
Montgomery Center, Vermont

Seafood, pasta and steaks at reasonable prices in a casual atmosphere. Beers, too. Info: 802-326-4682

INSIDER TIPS
1) Lifts without lines: On the weekend, take the triple. On weekdays, all lines are short or nonexistent.

2) Lifts to take to follow the sun: In the morning, the Jet and the Bonny are where it's at. In the afternoon, stay on the Bonny or take the tram to the summit.

3) What to read to find coupons deals: The *St. Albans Messenger* and *Boston Phoenix*

4) Snow stashes: Fact is, Jay Peak is one giant powder stash. For the deepest powder hit Beyond Beaver Pond, Timbucktu and Canyon Land.

5) Parking secret: Best bet is to park in the second or third lot up from the main tram-side parking lot. It looks like a long walk, but you can ski down a secret path behind the Hotel Jay straight to the ticket booth.

6) Finest meal for the lowest fare: The Belfry Restaurant, 10 minutes from Jay, is very popular. The food is excellent, but the place can get crowded.

Mount Snow Resort
WEST DOVER, VERMONT

Mount Snow's greatest strength and greatest weakness can be summed up in a single word: location. Because of its position in southernmost Vermont, mere minutes from the Massachusetts border, Mount Snow is the closest big-mountain skiing available to cooped-up New York and Connecticut skiers. The problem is, on a snowy weekend, they're all there. That much business means the resort usually has plenty of cash on hand to build new lifts, construct a new slopeside hotel, and make serious amounts of snow and keep it all nicely groomed. It also means there will be serious crowds and a cafeteria so packed the stairwells are sometimes filled with hungry skiers balancing lunch trays on their knees. These extremes are caught in the crosshairs of *SKI* Magazine reader comments. "Easy to get to" and "congested," they remark in the same breath. "New lifts, excellent grooming," they note, but "busloads of people." Location aside, where Mount Snow really shines is variety. Its trails run down all sides of a long ridge stretching from the gentle slopes of Haystack Mountain (formerly a separate area), through

VITAL STATS

SUMMIT: 3,600 feet
VERTICAL DROP: 1,700 feet
SKIABLE ACRES: 176
BEGINNER: 22%
INTERMEDIATE: 49%
ADVANCED/EXPERT: 29%
SNOWMAKING: 75% coverage
AVG. ANNUAL SNOWFALL: 163 in.
LIFTS: 23; 4 quads, 10 triples, 4 doubles, 5 surface lifts
TERRAIN PARKS/HALFPIPES: 2 terrain parks, 2 halfpipes
INFO: 800-245-SNOW; www.mountsnow.com

101

Mount Snow's glades cover 137 acres of hand-cleared terrain.

the blue cruisers of Carinthia (formerly a separate area) to the fearsome steeps of Jaws (formerly Jaws of Death). In between, there's mogul mania beneath the Beartrap lift, sunny skiing on Sunbrook and night tubing and sledding on the front side of the mountain.

SKIING IT

The skiing at Mount Snow is comprised of primarily fast, fun cruisers, with a handful of more challenging runs. It doesn't have the super-steep trails of northern Vermont areas like Stowe or Mad River Glen, but with 1,700 feet of vertical it isn't wimpy either.

Early on a cold winter morning, you can find softer snow and sunshine over at the aptly named Sunbrook area, where blue runs such as Thanks Walt and Sunspot get your legs warm. After fresh snow, powder hounds should visit the North Face and ski the birches on Epiphany and The Plunge. If it's open, Ripcord is a steep run worth a try, too.

Like many ski resorts, Mount Snow gets crowded at the end of the day. Be especially careful to avoid runs in the center of the hill, particularly below the Yankee Clipper quad. And skip casting a shadow on Long John, the narrow mountain road that funnels many beginners down from the summit; the traffic there is worse than rush hour on Manhattan's West Side Highway.

One More Time, which ends at the base, tends to be empty, but with good reason. It's narrow and often icy. A better bet is Snowdance, a super-wide cruiser that is rarely crowded even as happy hour approaches. Another good option is South Bowl to Tramline to Ego Alley. The snow is soft, the runs wide and very few people seem to know about it.

And, of course, there are trees: 137 acres of terrain in 12 separate areas, to be precise. All those are black diamond and one is double black–The Plunge. For challenge in the woods, there's plenty to choose from, which is indicative of Mount Snow as a whole. Fans realize that the resort packs a lot into its smaller space. And fans of Mount Snow include snowboarders and new-school skiers–the resort has become fabled among the nose-ring-and-purple-hair crowd. Its Un Blanco Gulch snowboarding park was the first in the East; and the Inferno terrain park is where millions of viewers saw the raddest of the rad strut their stuff during the Winter X Games.–D.G.

FAMILY MATTERS

As is the case with all American Skiing Company resorts, the kids' ski programs here work like a franchise. Daycare is available for kids as young as six weeks, and ski school, with a variety of all-day, part-day, or multiday programs, is for all ages.

Snow Camp is the answer for kids who are new to skiing. It's divided into small groups of children, based on both ability and age. Those groups hang tight, allowing the children to ski together, play together, and bond for their stay. Instructors stick with the same group, giving the kids a familiarity that makes them comfortable while skiing without mom or dad.

Older kids seven and up go to Mountain Camp and Mountain Riders and spend more of the day out on the mountain. The good news for parents is, because all the programs are based out of the Perfect Turns Discovery Center, it's relatively easy to track your kids down should you want to check in. The daycare, located in the heart of the base area, is easily accessible, too.

Kids don't have to settle for just skiing and boarding while at Mount Snow. The tubing park is open nightly. The Galaxy Arcade, located in the base lodge and open all day until 5 P.M., is just the type of place where 21st-century kids like to take a break (or spend the entire day). And there's more: The night lights up for free bring-your-own sledding (until 9 P.M.), ice skating (rentals available) and snowboarding on the 460-foot long "Gut" halfpipe (from 5 to 10 P.M.).

GETTING THERE

From Albany

Take I-90 to I-787 North to Route 7 East. Route 7 becomes Route 9 in Vermont. Take Route 9 East to Route 100 North. Follow to Mount Snow.

Drive Time: 1.5 hours

From Boston

Take Route 2 West to I-91 North to Exit 2. Take Route 9 West to Route 100 North. Follow to Mount Snow.

Drive Time: 2.5 hours

From New York City

Take I-95 North to I-91 North to Exit 2. Take Route 9 West to 100 North. Follow to Mount Snow.

Drive Time: 5 hours

LODGING

Grand Summit Resort Hotel

West Dover, Vermont

Steps away from the Summit Express lift, the Grand Summit features a full range of services including concierge, room service, bellman service, daily maid service, valet parking, 24-hour front desk, office services, ski check, laundry facilities and complete spa services with massages, salt scrubs, mud masks, wraps, paraffin treatments, facials, manicures and pedicures. Amenities include a large year-round outdoor heated pool, two outdoor hot tubs, a steam room, a sauna, a video arcade, a deli, Harriman's Restaurant and Pub, a retail shop and a health club. Accommodations range from hotel rooms to studios to three-bedroom units to a penthouse that sleeps 10. All rooms have a TV and VCR; most have fully equipped kitchens with refrigerators and dishwashers. Some deluxe rooms have fireplaces. Info: 800-451-4211; www.mountsnow.com (offers internet-only vacation specials)

Mount Snow Condos

West Dover, Vermont

Slopeside or within walking distance, there's a wide variety of condos to choose from. Lower Seasons units are a short walk to the slopes. Upper Seasons units are slopeside. Snowtree and Snow Mountain Village

Ride Haystack Mountain for wide, uncrowded cruisers.

units are in the base area, a short walk or shuttle to the lifts. All have fireplaces, washers and dryers, cable TV/VCRs and full kitchens with dishwashers and microwaves. Each complex has an amenities center with a pool and hot tub. Info: 800-451-4211; www.mountsnow.com (offers internet-only vacation specials)

Snow Lake Lodge
West Dover, Vermont

With a lakeside setting that offers spectacular views of Mount Snow, this lodge features 90 rooms, the Lakeside Bar and Grille, indoor and outdoor hot tubs, a corner store and a complimentary shuttle to lifts. Suites have small refrigerators. Info: 800-451-4211

The Mountaineer Inn
West Dover, Vermont

The Mountaineer is a charming family-owned and operated inn at the base of Mount Snow. All 27 guestrooms have private baths and are non-smoking. Features include hot tubs, fieldstone fireplaces, an in-home theater, a pool table, spacious sunny lounges, pianos, a cozy library, a comfortable BYOB bar and Ping-Pong. The inn is walking distance to the ski lifts, entertainment, nighttime halfpipe, ice skating and sledding. Free shuttle service is also available. Info: 802-464-5404

Austin Hill Inn
West Dover, Vermont

At The Austin Hill Inn you'll find a genuine "get away from it all" spirit, one that lets you be sensitive to the beauty of nature, curl up by a fireplace with a good book, or just clear your mind for creative pondering. The 11 distinctive guest rooms (many with balconies and fireplaces) and common rooms with fireplaces offer an individual character with a traditional feel. Info: 800-332-RELAX

DINING
Julie's Cafe and Julio's Wood-Fired Pizza
West Dover, Vermont

A passion for hot peppers and pastry diverted Julie Wilson from a career in nursing to one as a restaurateur. At Julie's Cafe, she has developed a new form of cuisine: Italian/Tex-Mex. Don't scoff. The hybrid works amazingly well in the wild mushroom crostini that comes zapped with a dab of chipotle adobo sauce. It's no less apparent in a chunk of seasoned, grilled salmon that meets its ideal mate in a sprightly fig salsa. Unassuming from the outside, this little roadhouse near Mount Snow packs an interior of considerable panache with its dramatic open kitchen and a deli counter, where the knockout desserts, such as volcanic mud pie, cocoa-dusted tiramisu and light lemon macaroon pie, reside. With the cafe's success, Wilson recently opened Julio's Wood-Fired Pizza next door, where the organic pies range from classic tomato-and-cheese to the Southwestern, a pie decked with black beans and green chilies. Guests are also welcome to design their own pies. Info: 802-464-2078 –S.M.

Maple Leaf Malt & Brewing Co.
Wilmington, Vermont

John Foote is the kind of beer lover who began brewing his own five-gallon batches in college. Maple Leaf Malt & Brewing Co., a handsome boutique operation housed in Wilmington's original general store, is not only his dream come true—it's a continuation of family tradition. His roots in the area go back four generations, and his uncle, a local baker, helped develop a menu that backs Foote's half-dozen brews beautifully. The enormous Brewery Bratwurst Platter, served with a heap of hot German potato salad, is stewed in Deerfield Valley Dark stout. That same ale imparts a pleasant kick to the Vermont cheddar–topped baked stuffed portobello.

Teetotalers and children can enjoy Maple Leaf's own craft-brewed root beer. Most patrons, though, are only too happy to congregate at the bar by the ingenious maple-trunk tap. Info: 802-464-9900 –S.M.

INSIDER TIPS

1) Lifts without lines: The Nitro Express quad usually moves smoothly, and both the North Face triple and the Challenger triple are rarely overcrowded. The Sunbrook quad is another good bet. The best advice, though, is to head over to Haystack where you'll normally ski right onto to the lift after each run.

2) Lifts to take to follow the sun: During the morning, until about noon or so, the sun is right above the Grand Summit Express quad on the main face. After noon, the Sunbrook quad is the place.

3) What to read to find coupons and deals: *Deerfield Valley News, Mount Snow Valley Chamber Guide, Brattleboro Reformer, Bennington Banner, Keene Sentinel,* and *Metroland.*

4) Snow stashes: Usually the trees. For intermediates and below, The Fantasticks. For better skiers, The Trials on the North Face. The Enchanted Forest, a.k.a. The Witches, at Haystack is usually stuffed with snow, too.

5) Parking secret: Parking is an issue everywhere, but you can't go wrong parking at the Carinthia area.

6) Finest meal for the lowest fare: The Roadhouse. It's a country-casual dining experience about four miles from the mountain on Route 100.

Okemo Mountain Resort

LUDLOW, VERMONT

Nearly 600,000 skiers visit Okemo every year, making it one of the most popular ski areas in New England. Skiers have come to rely on Okemo for acres and acres of mellow corduroy (no matter what the New England weather throws at it), on runs like Dream Weaver, Mountain Road, South

Face and Beginner Basin. Among its strengths, Okemo counts not only its wealth of modern slopeside condos but also its proximity to the vintage Vermont village of Ludlow, an emerging beauty with many lovely Victorian-era homes. Among Okemo's weaknesses are high prices and crowds, both on the hill and at the base. "The access road is too congested," says one *SKI* Magazine reader. "As for the base lodge," says another *SKI* reader, "get in, get out, and don't go back till it's time to go!" There was also the predictable refrain of "too flat, lacks challenge." The Jackson Gore expansion helped quell these complaints. Now skiers can wind their way down Okemo's fifth peak on 16 new intermediate and advanced trails serviced by four new lifts and a gondola. Narrower and more New England-esque than the resort's standard wide-open terrain, these slopes won't let skiers settle into cruise control. The Jackson Gore expansion adds over 30% in skiable terrain and handles one third of Okemo's visitors. Just as importantly, a substantial village development is up and running, with a slopeside hotel, shops and restaurants. —S.C.

VITAL STATS

SUMMIT: 3,344 feet

VERTICAL DROP: 2,150 feet

SKIABLE ACRES: 520

BEGINNER: 25%

INTERMEDIATE: 50%

ADVANCED/EXPERT: 25%

SNOWMAKING: 95% coverage

AVG. ANNUAL SNOWFALL: 200 in.

LIFTS: 14; 7 quads, 3 triples, 4 surface lifts

TERRAIN PARKS/HALFPIPES: 4 terrain parks, 2 halfpipes

INFO: 802-228-4041; www.okemo.com

SKIING IT

Okemo's snow is usually smooth as silk, groomed more meticulously than Wayne Newton's coif before a big show. And the lifts are top notch.

Ambitious skiers who catch the 8 A.M. chair can rack up a good 7,000 feet of prime vertical before the masses hit. If you happen to be among those later arrivals, know that Okemo's burgeoning popularity means tactical planning is required to avoid lift lines during peak times, especially between 9 and 10:30 A.M. Avoiding crowds at Okemo can be like trying to score first tracks at Squaw Valley, California—difficult but doable.

When riding either of the two fixed-grip South Ridge quads away from the base area, you'll have a sky-high view of the various lift mazes. Pay close attention. If the popular Northstar high-speed quad is jammed, there are two alternatives. You can either peel off above Northstar and catch the uppermost lift—the Black Ridge triple—or keep going past Northstar to the

Okemo's trails are meticulously groomed.

Sachem lift, a fixed-grip quad. Either route gets you quickly to the edges of Okemo, where trails and lifts remain uncrowded the longest.

Even though the high-speed lifts on both the South Face and Solitude terrain pods draw skiers like ants to a picnic, there's rarely more than a 10-minute wait. If Okemo is really rocking, the Green Ridge triple is a great safety valve. It's an older lift that most snow-sliders avoid, though it services some of the mountain's most entertaining, well-pitched cruisers, including Timberline, Sapphire and Tomahawk.

If you opt to spend time on the long, open cruisers off Solitude Express, don't ski below the day lodge. The trails there are mostly beginner runs laid out to access up-market homes and condos built in recent years. Kids may demand a run anyway, since it means skiing through a tunnel, but be warned: the ride back up is a slow one. The Jackson Gore expansion is definitely worth checking out, and as trails are added, the skiing there will get progressively more interesting—and challenging.

FAMILY MATTERS

Okemo's terrain alone makes it an ideal place for families. The skiing is gentle and offers a safe and fun way down for every level of skier. The ski school delivers too, offering classes for the littlest of tykes to race-ready teens. Kids can be dropped off all day and fed lunch, or take classes by the hour.

Little ones are well taken care of in the Penguin Playground Daycare Center, which ambitiously offers a one-hour "intro to skiing" program for three and four year olds. Novice SKIwee kids have their own segregated learning slope and lift.

If you want to sneak a peek at your kids while in ski school, Okemo makes it easy. Just check the big trail map in the learning center. It's color-coded to show where different ability levels will be skiing.

For adult fun, Okemo offers "parents' night off." On Saturdays and holidays, from 6 to 10 P.M. kids enjoy pizza and a movie while parents do as they feel–dine out elegantly, take in some après, or (imagine this!) just relax back in the condo on their own. For teens, the hangout is Altitude After Dark, a nonalcoholic nightspot open Saturday evenings with contests, moonlight volleyball and a DJ spinning tunes.

What also makes Okemo so popular for families is its 800-plus slopeside condos. Say what you will about condomania, but young families do best when there's a kitchen for snacks and quick breakfasts, room to spread out and play with games and toys, and easy access for midday naps.

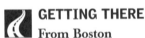
GETTING THERE
From Boston
Take Route 2 West to I-91 North to Exit 6. Take VT 103 North to Okemo.

Drive Time: 3 hours

From New York
Take I-95 North to I-91 North to Exit 6. Take VT 103 North to Okemo.

Drive Time: 4.5 hours

LODGING
Okemo Slopeside Lodging
Okemo Mountain Lodge, Kettle Brook, Winterplace, Solitude Village and Ledgewood condominiums offer luxury and convenience with direct ski-in–ski-out access to Okemo. The Okemo Resort Shuttle gives easy access Okemo Mountain's other condominium complexes, the base-lodge area and the Okemo Valley Golf Club and Nordic Center. Info: Okemo Mountain Resort Properties, 800-78-OKEMO

The Inn at Water's Edge
Ludlow, Vermont
With the children grown, New Yorkers Tina and Bruce Verdrager reno-

vated their rambling Victorian vacation home on the edge of Echo Lake into a country inn. Bruce's natural enthusiasm and Tina's culinary skills made it an instant success. Arriving guests are welcomed with a drink in the English pub, which is dominated by an authentic 100-year-old English bar of etched and leaded glass set in mahogany. Bruce tells of how he found it in Savannah, Georgia, of all places, while he minds the bar. Tina buzzes in and out of the kitchen, bringing in hors d'oeurves and preparing an elaborate three-course dinner. The kitchen remains open until the last guest arrives. "How can you let people drive all the way here and not give them dinner?" Tina asks. Though smallish, guestrooms are delightful and include breakfast and dinner. They're individually decorated with antiques, as are the two living rooms, which provide an alternative to the pub and game room. Nothing is fussy—just welcoming, like a visit to grandma's. And Tina's cooking—appetizers such as scallops in puff pastry with mustard sauce, entrées such as maple-glazed salmon and multi-course breakfasts—puts even grandma's to shame. Info: 802-228-8143 or 888-706-9736; www.innatwatersedge.com —H.N.

Echo Lake Inn
Ludlow, Vermont

This rambling, three-story, gabled inn looks just as a Vermont country inn should: white clapboards and a full-length porch outside, country furnishings and a big fireplace inside. It's big, warm and inviting, with nothing fancy but the food, which is where the Echo Lake excels. The creative continental fare includes appetizers such as pumpkin ravioli—poached, then simmered in a light Parmesan-and-chive cream—and entrées such as fresh rainbow trout sautéed with sun dried tomatoes, scallions, artichoke hearts, tomatoes and pine nuts. Upstairs, the guest rooms are furnished with a mishmash of country pieces, from near-antique to near-modern. Kids are welcome here, and the inn has family suites as well as a hot tub. Reservations are recommended. Info: 802-228-8602, 800-356-6844 —H.N.

The Governor's Inn
Ludlow, Vermont

This quaint inn offers nine rooms with private baths, Victorian flair, puffy comforters and a simply lovely setting just one mile from Okemo. The den is always alive with tea and Mozart and après-ski munchies.

Okemo's superpipe is serviced by its own lift.

There's gourmet dining on site as well, and the bed-and-breakfast or full-meal plan makes it affordable. Info: 800-GOVERNOR, 802-228-8830

The Golden Stage Inn
Proctorsville, Vermont

The Golden Stage Inn offers over 200 years of hospitality heritage. The 10 comfortable and plush rooms all have private baths. The fireside room is a great place to relax with a glass of wine. Four miles from Okemo, it is on the shuttle route, near snowmobile trails, and has snowshoeing trails right out the back door. Full breakfast and dinner plans are available. Info: 802-226-7744, 800-253-8226; www.goldenstageinn.com

DINING
Al Dentes
Ludlow, Vermont

Very affordable Italian cuisine. Breakfast, lunch and dinner are served daily. Info: 802-228-7400

Archie's Prime Time Steakhouse
Ludlow, Vermont

If you're a meat eater, specifically of the steak-and-burger kind, Archie's is a safe bet. With hand-cut prime steaks and prime rib, fresh seafood, Angus burgers, specialty sandwiches and a sizable salad bar, it's a place where big appetites won't go hungry. Archie's is also a dedicated sports bar with big-screen TVs and drink and lunch specials. So if you don't want to miss the Giants game after (or, perhaps, during) a day of skiing, this is your spot. Info: 802-228-3003

Art of the Chicken
Ludlow, Vermont

Catering to the poultry aficionado, this is a restaurant that subscribes to the "good meal at a fair price" school of cooking–and succeeds. Fried chicken, roasted chicken, chicken fingers, teriyaki chicken, chicken noodle soup, all manner of chicken salads, chicken lettuce and tomato sandwiches and chicken wings done up buffalo style are all tasty. Dine in or take out. Info: 802-228-7180

Cappuccino Restaurant
Ludlow, Vermont

They do serve a mean cappuccino, which is a good thing, since you will quite likely need a little pick-me-up after gorging from the mostly Italian menu. Crab cakes, escargot and shrimp cocktails get things going on the appetizer menu, and the entrée list includes both a wide selection of nicely prepared meats (duck, steak, chicken, fish and veal) as well as a long list of pastas. Cappuccino's also has a list of nightly specials, which might include rack of lamb, pine nut crusted Tilapia, steamed mussels and grilled portobello. The restaurant has a bright, airy atmosphere, the porch area even more so. Info: 802-228-7566

The Castle
Ludlow, Vermont

Built by European craftsmen for a past governor of Vermont, the Castle is more accurately described as a mansion that today offers one of the more regal dining settings near Okemo (it also has ten guest rooms) with excellent entrées. Info: 802-226-7361

Charaktors American Bar & Grill

Charaktors is like many other Northeast ski-town restaurant-bars: Energetic with classic, can't-miss American cuisine. You'll wobble out the door satisfied and full. The bar also has live music. Info: 802-226-4220

Crows Corner Bakery Cafe
Proctorsville, Vermont

Breakfast, lunch and desserts are available at this cafe that opens at 6 A.M. Tuesdays through Saturdays. It opens at 8 A.M. on Sundays and doesn't open at all on Mondays. They also serve a wide variety of teas and juices. Info: 802-226-7736

A State of Bean
Ludlow, Vermont

Ludlow's original coffee house offers delicious coffee and coffee drinks. Open seven days a week, serving breakfast and lunch. It's also home of the Big Chair Philosopher's Acoustic Music Series, a chance to hear the up-and-coming Bob Dylans of Vermont. Info: 802-228-BEAN

The Loft Tavern
Ludlow, Vermont

Though it depreciatingly refers to itself as the "home of warm beer, grumpy owner and lousy food," the Loft is a must stop for après ski. This Ludlow sports bar actually has cold beer and satisfying nachos, wings, hearty burgers and specials. You can judge the owner's grumpiness when and if you get the chance to meet him. Info: 802-228-5638

 EVENTS

Okemo Cares & Shares with Toys and Turkeys Food Drive Day

The first Sunday each December, Okemo invites you to bring three nonperishable fixings for a turkey dinner, a new child's toy, or a new clothing item to the ticket window and ski or ride for just $25. Special events and prizes trailside all day long.

National Safety Awareness Week at Okemo

Sponsored by the National Ski Areas Association, this weeklong event focuses on safety with children's clinics, safety lectures and helmet demos. Okemo also holds a fireworks display, a torchlight parade and moonlight snowshoeing expeditions. Held mid to late January.

Sugar on Snow Celebration

Sample some of Vermont's finest locally made maple syrup served up on

Okemo's natural snow. Free samples and demonstrations all day long. Held in mid February.

Chuck and Huck Dummy Big Air

Held on the "teen Saturday" in April, this event involves contestants building their own dummy on skis or snowboard and sending it over a jump. Dummy (and owner) receive prizes for originality and style points.

INSIDER TIPS

1) Lifts without lines: Skip the Northstar Express on weekends and holidays and instead ride the Black Ridge triple to the Green Ridge triple. Another secret combo is to ride the Sachem quad to the Glades Peak quad and head to the South Face Area to ski glades and long cruisers minus the crowds.

2) Lifts to take to follow the sun: Make your way over to the South Face Area first thing in the morning. Around noontime, head to either the Northstar quad or Green Ridge triple. The Solitude Peak and Morning Star areas get the afternoon sunshine.

3) What to read to find coupons and deals: The best source for winter coupons and discounts is www.okemo.com. Check the banner ads, they change regularly. Also, *The Message for the Week* and *Black River Tribune.*

4) Snow stashes: Gladed trails like Double Diamond, Outrage, Forrest Bump and Loose Spruce are typically hiding snow. Defiance, Sel's Choice, Searle's Way, Fast Lane, Punch Line, The Narrows and Whistler can often yield some bounty, too.

5) Parking secret: Here, the "early bird" rule definitely applies. The Loft parking lot is the best, but the smartest bet is to take advantage of the shuttles, which start running at 7:30 A.M.

6) Finest meal for the lowest fare: Al Dentes.

THE BEST OF THE REST OF VERMONT

Ascutney Mountain Resort

BROWNSVILLE, VERMONT

Best known as a family mountain—if known at all—Ascutney had always lurked at the edge of the New England skier's consciousness as that place on the east edge of Vermont, off by itself in the Connecticut River Valley. Then it abruptly raised its profile, quite literally, by installing a new high-speed quad, the North Peak Express, which carries skiers almost 300 feet higher up Mount Ascutney and opens up a half dozen black diamond trails. Somehow, the difference between 1,500 vertical feet and 1,800 vertical feet is enough to pique one's interest.

In fact, since 1993, Ascutney owners Steve and Susan Plausteiner have invested millions of dollars for capital improvements. In addition to the North Peak expansion, the resort has increased snowmaking coverage from approximately 60 percent to 95 percent of total terrain, added a new surface lift in its 10-acre learning area, completed major upgrades to hotel and condominium units, created new tree-skiing areas, and erected a new lodge and dedicated learning area just for kids. As anyone who has visited recently will attest, Ascutney's growth spurt has proven a success.

VITAL STATS

SUMMIT: 2,520 feet
VERTICAL DROP: 1,800 feet
SKIABLE ACRES: 150
BEGINNER: 30%
INTERMEDIATE: 40%
ADVANCED/EXPERT: 30%
SNOWMAKING: 95% coverage
AVG. ANNUAL SNOWFALL: 175 in.
LIFTS: 6; 1 quad, 3 triples, 1 double, 1 surface lift
TERRAIN PARKS/HALFPIPES: 1 terrain park, 1 halfpipe
INFO: 800-243-0011; www.ascutney.com

GETTING THERE
From Woodstock

Take Route 106 South to Route 44 East. Follow to Ascutney Mountain Resort.

Drive Time: .5 hour

From Boston

Take Route 2 West to I-91 North to Exit 8. Take Route 131 to Route 5.

Ascutney Mountain added 300 vertical feet with the North Peak expansion.

Turn left onto Route 44A to Route 44. Follow to Ascutney Mountain Resort.
Drive Time: 2.5 hours

From New York City
Take I-95 North to I-91 North to Exit 8. Take Route 131 to Route 5.
Turn left onto Route 44A to Route 44. Follow to Ascutney Mountain Resort.
Drive Time: 4 hours

Bromley Mountain Resort
PERU, VERMONT

Known for its sunny days, easy access (right beside Vermont's Route 11)
and family-friendliness, Bromley is now gaining a reputation for afford-
ability. Tickets cost an average of 20 percent less than at the East's bigger
resorts, and the widely acclaimed children's programs are up to 50 percent
less expensive. Though short on slopeside amenities, Bromley has "access
to great food, shopping and nightlife," in one *SKI* Magazine reader's esti-
mation. Still, another *SKI* reader complains that you "must travel to
Manchester for those"—a six-mile trip. Once called Big Bromley, the resort
is now considered small—or, from one *SKI* reader's point of view, "not so
big you lose the kids." The mountain is also thought of—mistakenly—as
merely a playground for intermediates. It's all that, but most of the resort's
east side is black-diamond terrain, with "some good gnarly trails," says one

SKI reader. After a snowstorm, powder can lay deep and remarkably untouched well into the afternoon on expert runs such as Havoc and Stargazer. Bromley is "skiing the way it used to be," observes one *SKI* reader, and this is obvious from the old rambling base lodge. But what the lodge lacks in ambience, the staff makes up for with friendliness–they ask how you are and actually listen to your answer. On the mountain, readers praise the old-style, winding narrow trails as well as the wide-open slopes: the "best of both worlds," says one. But others complain that the resort "needs more terrain." Still, with curbside drop-off, Bromley offers what one reader calls a "no-hassle ski experience," even if you do have to schlep your stuff up a flight of stairs first. The best time to ski the south-facing Sun Mountain is midweek: Tickets are cheap and crowds nonexistent. With few others on your tail, you'll have time to soak in the "exquisite view from the summit" before making tracks on either freshly laid corduroy or powder.

VITAL STATS

SUMMIT: 3,284 feet

VERTICAL DROP: 1,334 feet

SKIABLE ACRES: 300

BEGINNER: 35%

INTERMEDIATE: 34%

ADVANCED/EXPERT: 31%

SNOWMAKING: 80% coverage

AVG. ANNUAL SNOWFALL: 145 in.

LIFTS: 10; 2 quads, 4 doubles, 4 surface lifts

TERRAIN PARKS/HALFPIPES: 1 terrain park, 1 halfpipe

INFO: 802-824-5522; www.bromley.com

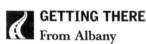 GETTING THERE
From Albany

Take I-90 East to Route 787 to Route 7 East. Route 7 becomes Route 9 in Vermont. Take Route 9 East to Route 7 North to Exit 4. Take Route 11/30 East to Bromley.

Drive Time: 1.5 hours

From Boston

Take Route 2 West to I-91 North to Exit 6. Take Route 103 North to Route 11 West to Bromely.

Drive Time: 3 hours

From New York City

Take I-95 North to I-91 North to Exit 6. Take Route 103 North to Route 11 West to Bromely.

Drive Time: 4 hours

Burke Mountain

EAST BURKE, VERMONT

There may be no view more beautiful than the one you get atop Burke Mountain. Through the clear air of Vermont's remote Northeast Kingdom, skiers get off the Willoughby quad and gaze out across a vast, open landscape of rolling hills and meadows northward to the region's geographic signature, the thousand-foot rock walls of Willoughby Gap. At your feet is a mountain that will pleasantly surprise you. You won't find high-speed quads and tubing parks, but you will find 45 fun and exciting ways down 2,000 vertical feet of pure mountain. Burke may lack some of the bells and whistles, but it has all the skiing you need.

There are two parts to the ski area. The lower mountain is a self-contained family area, with the base lodge, the Sherburne double, the J-bar and five easy runs pitched just right for beginners and intermediates. It's fun, safe and just seconds away from the lodge and a cup of hot cocoa. The real skiing is on the upper mountain, served by the Willoughby quad (wicked slow) and the Mountain Poma (wicked fast).

The upper mountain is a maze of trails that crisscross their way down 1,500 feet of sustained north-facing vertical. Most of the runs are challenging cruisers that curve and dive and bend, with terrain variations to keep you entertained and alert. Even after five runs on the same trail, you can find a new line, a new way to ski each corner. There are some true expert trails scattered across the upper mountain. Wilderness, Ledges, Fox's Folly and Doug's Drop are just a few, with plenty of bumps, steeps and drop-offs.

VITAL STATS

SUMMIT: 3,267 feet

VERTICAL DROP: 2,000 feet

SKIABLE ACRES: 180

BEGINNER: 25%

INTERMEDIATE: 45%

ADVANCED/EXPERT: 30%

SNOWMAKING: 75% coverage

AVG. ANNUAL SNOWFALL: 250 in.

LIFTS: 4; 1 quad, 1 double, 2 surface lifts

TERRAIN PARKS/HALFPIPES: 1 terrain park, 1 halfpipe

INFO: 802-626-3322; www.skiburke.com

Burke Mountain Academy racers train daily, using the Poma to ski on Warren's Way and Big Dipper. Take a moment to watch them: You'll learn a thing or two. Burke was the first—and is still one of the best—race/prep schools in the country. It has nurtured some of the nation's most successful racers, including five competitors in the Salt Lake 2002 Olympics. The Academy also now owns the long-suffering resort, having bought it two years ago to ensure its future.

There are three things that you have to do when you ski Burke. The first is to rip some fast turns down Big Dipper, which was recently widened. It's FIS-sanctioned for world-class racing and has four distinct headwalls that will quicken your pulse and put a smile on your face. Second, find your way into Burke's woods. There are 11 gladed trails (marked, but officially nameless on the trail map) that are worth every second. The trees are close enough to make it challenging, but wide enough for you to ski nonstop if your reflexes and legs can take it. Last, make the effort to get to East Bowl. It's a long trail (2.25 miles), narrow, and an adventure every time down. Ski it in the morning when the sun lights it up beautifully, and let your boards run.

Burke isn't a ritzy resort, but you won't lack for a couple of good places to stay. One, the Inn at Mountain View Farm, was a state-of-the-art dairy farm and creamery in the late 1800s. Now it's a beautifully restored country inn on 440 acres of ridgeline fields and forest. At the Vermont Inn, you'll think you've stepped back in time at an English country manor. Its rooms are filled with antiques, floral patterns and hand-stitched quilts.

For dinner, you'll have been sure to make reservations at River Garden Cafe in the heart of the village. Arrive a little early for a drink at the bar—they make a mean martini. The place is popular with both locals and tourists, and for good reason. One of the owners is a veteran of the New York City restaurant scene. The most common nightlife in East Burke involves a good book by the fire and a farm video for the kids. But many people suggest moonlit snowshoeing on the Kingdom Trails system, which offers 50 miles of interconnected trails for snowshoeing or Nordic skiing. —D.L. and K.L.

 GETTING THERE

From Boston

Take Route 2 West to I-91 North to Exit 23. Follow signs to Burke Mountain.

Drive Time: 3 hours

From Hartford

Take I-91 North to Exit 23. Follow signs to Burke Mountain.

Drive Time 3.5 hours

Cochran's Ski Area

RICHMOND, VERMONT

Cochran's is two things. To anyone with a passion for the sport of ski racing, it is as hallowed as any church. These are the slopes that the late Mickey Cochran carved out of the north-facing hills behind his farmhouse, and on which he coached his children—"The Flying Cochrans"—to the pinnacle of their sport. But more importantly, Cochran's is a snowy hill with a couple of surface lifts on it, where young Vermonters who might not otherwise have the chance can still learn the joy of bombing down the hill much too fast for their mothers' comfort.

In its smallness, Cochran's is a throwback. Many Vermont communities once had little ski areas of their own. They were break-even propositions, run by the Jaycees or the Outing Club—a rope tow on a hill at the edge of town, often with no lodge and certainly no snowmaking. But their humbleness belied their importance. Such slopes were the cradle of skiing's golden years, where a generation learned to ski. Their beauty was their smallness, their closeness to home, their inexpensiveness, and, most of all, their sense of community.

They were also a parent's best friend, as Cochran's is today. You can still park within 50 yards of the lift, boot up at your car, and be skiing in a few minutes. A family season's pass costs $250, so when your littlest one's enthusiasm flags after two or three hours, there's no economic necessity to stick it out. Older kids don't need you around at all: Drop them off with a few of their friends and they'll find their own fun while you run errands.

There are two tows that service the upper slopes at Cochran's. If you're lucky, the rope tow will be running. It runs parallel to the T-bar, and is as fast as the T-bar is poky. When it's operating, skiers cycle at an astonishing clip, logging run after run at 350 vertical feet apiece. The six trails have just enough pitch to reach race speed if you care to. But in this age of round-the-clock grooming, the most remarkable aspect of skiing at Cochran's is

VITAL STATS

SUMMIT: 1,000 feet

VERTICAL DROP: 500 feet

SKIABLE ACRES: 30

BEGINNER: 22%

INTERMEDIATE: 56%

ADVANCED/EXPERT: 22%

SNOWMAKING: 20% coverage

AVG. ANNUAL SNOWFALL: 88 in.

LIFTS: 4 surface lifts

TERRAIN PARKS/HALFPIPES:
no terrain parks, no halfpipes

INFO: 802-434-2479;
www.cochranskiarea.com

the undulation of the surface beneath your skis. The snow cover, which packs down to no more than a foot in the best of winters (and sometimes as little as two or three inches), actually follows the contours of the hillside beneath it. The bumps and rolls surprise you, and keep you alert. Yes, the cover is thin in places, and at first you'll fear for your skis' edges. Then you realize that it's grass showing through, not rocks. Mickey was nothing if not meticulous about his trails. He coddled that hillside, guarding against erosion (no mountain bikes allowed), knowing that rocks will hurt a ski's metal edge, but a little grass won't.

Cochran's survival as a community slope is heartening, though it is symbolic at best. The days of community hills are gone. Pampered modern-day customers have been trained to insist on high-speed quads, homogenized slopes, and never-ending acres of terrain. Cochran's is an anomaly, a bit of a functioning museum. It's hard to visit there without a tinge of nostalgia, a homesickness for the slopes of your youth.

But your wistfulness is lost on the children clinging to the orange bars on the Mighty Mite tow. All they know is that Cochran's exists, and skiing is fun. In that, there's solace. –J.C.

 GETTING THERE
From Burlington

Take I-89 West to Exit 11. Take Route 2 South to Bridge Street. Turn left on Cochran Road and follow to ski area.

Drive Time: 1 hour

Mad River Glen
WAITSFIELD, VERMONT

In the minds of most people, Mad River Glen is an anachronism, a working museum of skiing the way it used to be. To its devotees, however, it's a shrine to skiing as it ought to be, a place with little snowmaking, limited grooming and slow-as-molasses lifts, where you ski the hand that Mother Nature deals you. Often, that translates into spotty conditions and even extended periods during which much of the mountain is unskiable. But when the weather cooperates, Mad River can serve up Western-style powder for weeks—if not months—on end, leaving your skis tracks deep in untracked fluffies. Because Mad River has one of the ski industry's most loyal followings (you've probably seen the red and white MAD RIVER GLEN: SKI IT IF YOU CAN bumper sticker on many a rusted-out Subaru), and everyone else tends to just stay away, it's no surprise that the *SKI* Magazine readers that do have something to say about the mountain find almost no weaknesses and plenty to rave about: "They put the adventure back in skiing"; "the black diamonds really mean expert"; "steep, natural, empty"; "real skiing without the glitz." And all those assessments are true. Owned and run as a co-op, Mad River feels like a multi-generational commune. Strangers chat in the lift-lines, the lodge music is always groovy, and thigh-crushing trails descend narrow and silent, because the 1948 single chair—the only way to access the big peak other than skins or snow-shoes—blissfully limits the number of skiers on the mountain. Quirky, cantankerous and crazed as a Vermont farmer on hard cider, Mad River isn't for everyone and doesn't want to be. You'd better like bumps, because they don't groom the blacks. Mad River's signature run, Paradise, may very well be the toughest run in the East. And when Mother Nature is cranky, Mad River's trails suffer more than most. Still, the place is such a fabulous monument to what one *SKI* reader calls "ye olde New England skiing" that it ought to get a preservation grant from the National Endowment for the Humanities. (Indeed, Historic Landmark designation is already being discussed.) Anyone who likes chutes, trees, telemarking, cliff-jumping and the ultimate challenge should watch the snow reports: When powder hits the Greens of Vermont, ski Mad River—if you can.

VITAL STATS

SUMMIT: 3,637 feet
VERTICAL DROP: 2,037 feet
SKIABLE ACRES: 800
BEGINNER: 30%
INTERMEDIATE: 30%
ADVANCED/EXPERT: 40%
SNOWMAKING: 15% coverage
AVG. ANNUAL SNOWFALL: 250 in.
LIFTS: 4; 3 doubles, 1 single
TERRAIN PARKS/HALFPIPES:
  no terrain parks, no halfpipes
INFO: 802-496-3551;
  www.madriverglen.com

GETTING THERE
From Burlington

Take I-89 South to Route 2 South. Take Route 100 South to Route 17 West. Follow to Mad River Glen.

Drive Time: 1 hour

From Boston

Take I-93 North to I-89 North. Take Route 2 East to Route 100B to Route 100. Take Route 17 West to Mad River Glen.

Drive Time: 3.5 hours

From New York City

Take I-87 North to Exit 20 to Route 149 East. Route 149 East turns into Route 4 East in Vermont. Take Route 4 East over Sherburne Pass to Route 100 North. Take Route 17 West to Mad River Glen.

Drive Time: 5 hours

Suicide Six

WOODSTOCK, VERMONT

This modest Vermont resort—the cradle of North American lift-served skiing—is one of those rare patchwork-quilt creations where contrasting pieces produce a warm, harmonic whole. Skiers and riders, tourists and locals, families and adrenaline junkies all seem at home. Perhaps it's because the area has been around for so long— or the fact that it's a part of Laurence Rockefeller's four-star Woodstock Inn & Resort—that Suicide seems so adept at making all manner of guests feel comfortable.

"This is where it all started—where alpine skiing began as a commercial venture," explains Lenny Britton, director of the area's venerable junior race program. In 1934, America's first ski tow, powered by a Model-T engine, started running just down the ridgeline on a pasture called Gilbert's Hill. A year later, Bunny Bertram installed a lift on "Hill 6." Bertram, a young Dartmouth grad with an eye for terrain and an ear for alliteration, embraced the suggestion that it would be "suicide" to ski the north face of Hill 6, and named it Suicide Six.

Today, "The Face" is still a benchmark for experts, but a run down any

VITAL STATS

SUMMIT: 1,200 feet

VERTICAL DROP: 650 feet

SKIABLE ACRES: 100

BEGINNER: 30%

INTERMEDIATE: 40%

ADVANCED/EXPERT: 30%

SNOWMAKING: 50% coverage

AVG. ANNUAL SNOWFALL: 80 in.

LIFTS: 3; 2 doubles, 1 surface lift

TERRAIN PARKS/HALFPIPES: no terrain parks, 1 half-pipe

INFO: 802-457-6661; www.suicidesix.com

Suicide Six is named after a Dartmouth skier who was told it would be suicide to ski the north face of Hill 6.

portion of the area's untrammeled terrain is just as fulfilling. From the summit, novices and families dally along the enchanting Easy Mile. Intermediates cruise Bunny's Boulevard or wander through The Gully, with its incongruous high-alpine feel. For Warren Miller wannabes, Back Scratcher and Showoff are must skis.

And all roads lead to home. Parents have a comfort factor when they come here because all the trails come back to the lodge.

With an emphasis on comfort, the exclusive Woodstock Inn & Resort compounds the good feelings by offering free skiing–lessons and rentals included–to all of their midweek guests. And those lucky enough to visit on a Friday should be sure to take a long look up the mountain. That's when 500 local children are furloughed from school for an afternoon on the slopes. It's skiing's future, swarming the slopes of Suicide Six. –D.H.

GETTING THERE
From Boston

Take I-93 North to I-89 North to Exit 1. Take Route 4 West to Woodstock and follow signs to Suicide Six.

Drive Time: 3.5 hours

From New York City

Take I-95 North to I-91 North to I-89 North. Take Exit 1 to Route 4 West to Woodstock. Follow signs to Suicide Six.

Drive Time: 5.5 hours

Bolton Valley Resort

BOLTON VALLEY, VERMONT

"Bolton Valley," a friend once remarked, "feels more like skiing in the Alps than any other ski area in New England."

I'd always thought of the resort—a family favorite often forgotten among the giants of northern Vermont—as more Lilliputian than Alpine. But as I got to know it better, I began to see his point.

With the highest base elevation in Vermont and a tasteful mini-village of Bavarian-style architecture, Bolton feels a little like Lech, but at a fraction of the marks. Sure, skiing the meandering Sherman's Pass off the summit— or even Lost Boyz, a gladed double-black served by the resort's only modern quad—will never be confused with conquering the Hahnenkamm. But you won't hear any complaints from in-the-know families who gravitate to Bolton for its high-alpine beauty and low-brow pricing. As one Long Island skier told me, grinning between powder runs last year: "It's the kind of place that families back home would love—if they only knew it existed."

Part of the secret of Bolton is that it revels in all things small. With barely-there lift lines, all five chairlifts serve manageable novice trails, but there are enough blue squares to grow on, and even a few scary pitches off the summit. Meanwhile, the Mighty-Mite handle-tow, just out the back door of the ski-in–ski-out village, is perfect for tots.

Surrounded by some 5,000 pristine acres, Bolton is also brimming with tons of untapped backcountry potential. Just ask any of the bark-eating locals working the seams between the resort's three separate peaks.

There are other attractions: an extensive cross-country trail network, always well-covered thanks to its high elevation; spectacular views, north to Mt. Mansfield, south to Camel's Hump, west to Lake Champlain; night skiing (rare in Vermont); and proximity to Burlington (30 minutes). Lakeside Burlington is not only a lively town to visit après ski, but a convenient gateway, with low-cost flights from major

VITAL STATS

SUMMIT: 3,150 feet
VERTICAL DROP: 1,634 feet
SKIABLE ACRES: 165
BEGINNER: 27%
INTERMEDIATE: 47%
ADVANCED/EXPERT: 26%
SNOWMAKING: 80% coverage
AVG. ANNUAL SNOWFALL: 250 in.
LIFTS: 6; 1 quad, 4 doubles, 1 surface lift
TERRAIN PARKS/HALFPIPES: 1 terrain park, 1 halfpipe
INFO: 802-434-3444; www.boltonvalley.com

Bolton Valley's 60 trails cover 168 acres.

markets (New York's JFK and five Florida cities) via JetBlue Airlines.

Under the ownership of industry-veteran Bob Fries since October 2002, Bolton Valley has hefted its marketing and customer service efforts while making significant headway on facilities. True, not every facet is buffed yet. But frugal New Englanders—and the occasional wayward Austrian—will feel right at home. —D.H.

GETTING THERE

From Burlington

Take I-89 South to Exit 10 to Route 2 North. Follow To Bolton Valley Access Road.

Drive Time: .5 hour

From Boston

Take I-93 North to I-89 North. Take Route 2 North to Bolton Valley Access Road.

Drive Time: 3 hours

From New York City

Take I-95 North to I-91 North to I-89 North. Take Route 2 North to Bolton Valley Access Road.

Drive Time: 4.5 hours

Magic Mountain

LONDONDERRY, VERMONT

One word can sum up Magic Mountain: "steeps." The place has them, no question about it. Magic is often referred to as the Mad River Glen of southern Vermont, and for good reason. In addition to its humble infrastructure and a hard-core community of regulars, it has the only real, sustained pitch you'll find south of Killington. Over half of its 1,700-foot vertical drop legitimately rates black or double black, so expect to be challenged.

Magic runs a couple of diesel-fueled fixed-grip lifts and has limited snowmaking and grooming, so don't expect packed-powder corduroy every day of the season. But if you've got the legs—and the snow's coming down—there's no better place for expert skiing anywhere in southern Vermont.

From the top of the red chair, you'll have your pick of challenging glades like Twilight Zone or Goniff. Or you can launch yourself down Master Magician's 45-degree pitch. If you like the woods, check out the tasty cache between Wizard and Broomstick, which the locals keep nicely pruned. And for a truly "extreme" experience, Red Line has three rock bands that will make you stop before you drop. The upper part of Red Line is not technically even a "trail," but the credo at Magic is to let people ski where they want to—a kind of "go ahead and have fun" attitude that's refreshing in these times.

No, there aren't any high-speed lifts. But the double and triple chairs both access the summit, and there's no flat run-out at the bottom, so you'll get plenty of vertical.

Resorts like Mad River Glen have proven that you don't need detachable lifts for great skiing. The difference at Magic is that you won't find crowds of fanatics like those that choke Mad River on a powder day.

Until the snowmaking improves, it must be said that Magic's conditions can be hit or miss. But it's often worth the gamble, given that lift tickets cost considerably less than at nearby Stratton. The new owners promise

VITAL STATS

SUMMIT: 2,850 feet

VERTICAL DROP: 1,700 feet

SKIABLE ACRES: 135

BEGINNER: 25%

INTERMEDIATE: 36%

ADVANCED/EXPERT: 39%

SNOWMAKING: 87% coverage

AVG. ANNUAL SNOWFALL: 180 in.

LIFTS: 5; 1 triple, 2 doubles, 2 surface lifts

TERRAIN PARKS/HALFPIPES: no terrain parks, 1 halfpipe

INFO: 802-824-5645; www.magicmtn.com

Over half of Magic Mountain's 1,700-foot vertical rates black or double black.

that increased snowmaking and grooming are top priorities, and they plan to stay on it in the years to come. Those of us who live around here have our fingers crossed that they keep their promise. —E.V.

GETTING THERE
From Albany

Take I-90 East to Route 787 to Route 7 East. Route 7 becomes Route 9 in Vermont. Take Route 9 East to Route 7 North to Exit 4. Take Route 11/30 East to Magic Mountain.

Drive Time: 1.5 hours

From Boston

Take Route 2 West to I-91 North to Exit 6. Take Route 103 North to Route 11 West. Follow to Magic Mountain.

Drive Time: 3 hours

From New York City

Take I-95 North to I-91 North to Exit 6. Take Route 103 North to Route 11 West. Follow to Magic Mountain

Drive Time: 4 hours

Don't Miss: Gran' Ma Frisby's Restaurant, 5 minutes away on Route 11 (802-824 5931)